D1225905

SCOTTISH WRITERS

Editor

DAVID DAICHES

HUGH MACDIARMID

by Kenneth Buthlay

Kenneth Buthlay produced his first study of Hugh MacDiarmid in 1964, and it rapidly took its place as a classic presentation of MacDiarmid's progress and achievement as a poet. The present book is a completely revised and extended version of that, taking into account MacDiarmid's own writing between 1964 and his death in 1978 as well as earlier work that has only become accessible in this period and criticism of the poet that has appeared in recent years. The result is an illuminating account of MacDiarmid's development as a poet, with a careful examination of his sources, influences and motivating ideas and lively critical examination of individual poems and technical devices. It is both a comprehensive introduction to MacDiarmid and a help to further understanding for those who already know him.

HUGH MACDIARMID

KENNETH BUTHLAY

SCOTTISH ACADEMIC PRESS

EDINBURGH

Published by
Scottish Academic Press Ltd.
33 Montgomery Street, Edinburgh EH7 5JX

First published 1982
SBN 7073 0307 9

Printed in Great Britain by
Clark Constable Ltd., Edinburgh

CONTENTS

ACKNOWLEDGMENT

The Scottish Academic Press acknowledges the financial assistance of the Scottish Arts Council in the publication of this volume.

ABBREVIATED REFERENCES

References to MacDiarmid's *Complete Poems* are given throughout by page number only.

References which appear in abbreviated style are as follows:

A.	=	*Annals of the Five Senses.*
D.R.	=	*Daily Record.*
F.M.	=	*Free Man.*
G.H.	=	*Glasgow Herald.*
I.S.	=	*Irish Statesman.*
L.P.	=	*Lucky Poet.*
M.S.	=	*Modern Scot.*
N.A.	=	*New Age.*
N.R.	=	*Northern Review.*
N.S.	=	*New Statesman.*
R.A.	=	*Revue Anglo-Américaine.*
Sc.	=	*Scotsman.*
S.C.	=	*Scottish Chapbook.*
S.E.	=	*Selected Essays of Hugh MacDiarmid.*
S.E.J.	=	*Scottish Educational Journal.*
S.L.J.	=	*Scottish Literary Journal.*
S.M.	=	*Scots Magazine.*
S.O.	=	*Scots Observer.*
T.L.S.	=	*Times Literary Supplement.*

CHAPTER I

INTRODUCTION

Hugh MacDiarmid was born Christopher Murray Grieve on 11 August 1892, at Langholm in Dumfriesshire, close to the Scottish-English border. His father was a rural postman. On his mother's side of the family, his relatives tended to be farm workers; on his father's side, many of them worked in the local tweed mills.

For much of his boyhood the family was housed in the same building as the local library, and he borrowed books from it in vast quantities, using a clothes basket for the purpose. His schooling was at Langholm Academy, where one of his teachers was the composer Francis George Scott, later to set many of his poems to music and help him with practical criticism of his work. But his crucial mentor seems to have been George Ogilvie, principal English teacher at Broughton Junior Student Centre, Edinburgh, to which he proceeded at the age of sixteen, with the avowed intention of becoming a teacher himself.

Instead of teaching, he turned in 1910 to journalism. The sudden, unexpected death of his father, at the age of 47, occurred early in the following year. A series of newspaper jobs then took him to various parts of Scotland and to Wales, where his active political interests (he had joined the Independent Labour Party at the age of sixteen) brought him into contact with Keir Hardie. He had his first offering to the *New Age* accepted in 1911—"and I thought I had achieved world-wide fame"[1]—and in 1913 a Fabian committee acknowledged his assistance with research for a book on *The Rural Problem*.[2]

He joined the Royal Army Medical Corps in 1915, and saw service as a sergeant in Salonica, Italy and France, interrupted by treatment for bouts of malaria. In 1918 he married Margaret Skinner, who had been a copyholder in one of the newspaper offices where he had worked, and he was demobilised the following year.

He was soon to settle in Montrose, Angus, where he remained (apart from one period in the Highlands) until 1929, earning his living as a reporter on the local paper, becoming a town councillor and a J.P., and launching himself into an extraordinary welter of activities in the cause of what came to be known as the Scottish Renaissance movement. The prime products of that movement were his many books, from the first trial-run, *Annals of the Five Senses* by C. M. Grieve, in 1923, to the *Complete Poems of Hugh MacDiarmid*, published shortly after his death in 1978. Most of his work was deeply concerned with Scotland, or his vision, his idea of Scotland. He was as incensed by his countrymen's neglect of their native traditions as by their abrogation of responsibility for their own affairs, and he took it upon himself to "keep up perpetually a sort of Berserker rage" of protest, and to act as "the catfish that vitalizes the other torpid denizens of the aquarium."[3]

He was a founder-member of the Scottish Centre of PEN (1927) and of the National Party of Scotland (1928). His relations with Nationalist politicians were always stormy, particularly on the issue of his advocacy of a Social Credit programme, specially planned by Major C. H. Douglas, as the economic policy of an independent Scotland. This, and his growing leanings towards Communism, led to his expulsion from the National Party in 1933. He joined the Communist Party in the following year—and was before very long expelled from it in turn, for nationalist deviation—though he rejoined in a gesture of solidarity when the Party was at its lowest ebb, in 1956. He wore his contradictions like campaign medals, and battled on towards his own vision of the future, making his own myths along the way. These were eccentric, no doubt, but at least he saw clearly in advance that the orthodox myths of Great Britain and the Empire/Commonwealth were doomed. And one of the constant elements in his thinking should not be forgotten: his nationalism was always conceived as a necessary condition of internationalism. As he saw the issue, Scotland must regain her independence in order to contribute something of her own again to "the comity of nations."

In 1929 there began an unhappy stay in England, which may have had some bearing on his "anglophobia" (listed as his hobby in *Who's Who*). He went to London to work for Compton Mackenzie's pioneering radio magazine, *Vox*, and domestic and personal problems were soon compounded by unemployment when the magazine failed for lack of financial backing. The following year, he moved to Liverpool, to do publicity work for an organisation promoting the interests of Merseyside, but he lost that job and returned to London, becoming associated with a publishing firm. His foundering marriage ended in divorce and separation from his two children in 1932.

On his return to Scotland with his second wife, Valda Trevlyn, and their infant son, he tried to scrape a living by journalism in Edinburgh, but soon moved to Whalsay, in the Shetland Islands, where he remained in virtual exile, with occasional forays to the mainland, from 1933–1941. At least physical survival was less of a problem there, though he felt his long periods of isolation very acutely in other respects. His health was already precarious when he arrived in Shetland, and in 1935 he succumbed to a breakdown which necessitated a spell in a hospital near Perth.

Even during the long years on Whalsay, his enormous energy found ways of making itself felt in Scotland, but what mattered most, his poetry, found few outlets. Then the War brought him back under conscription to Glasgow in 1941, to a job as a fitter in the copper shell band department of an engineering works. From this he moved to service as an engineer on a ship engaged in estuarial duties.

At the War's end he was made redundant, and rejoined the unemployed. In 1950 he was awarded a Civil List pension of £150 a year. He moved soon afterwards to the farm worker's cottage near Biggar, in Lanarkshire, where he lived until his death at the age of eighty-six, on 9 September 1978. During this final period, recognition of his stature as a writer in Scotland grew mainly through the interest of younger writers, whether they followed up his leads (as many did) or not. Everybody found him too extreme, but he was nevertheless in touch with everybody. If one were to try to sum up his basic position in a phrase, it would be perhaps "an extremist on principle." Or as Edwin Muir put it, he was "everything that is out and out."[4]

From 1949 onwards he visited various Communist countries, and recognition at home was signalled by the award of an honorary LL.D. by Edinburgh University in 1957. But what he said was the real breakthrough came in 1962 with the publication in America of his *Collected Poems*: not by any means the volume that had been planned, but nevertheless a very substantial collection, which could hardly be overlooked or ignored. The gaps in this collection were finally filled, and an extensive section of mostly minor verse added, when his *Complete Poems* appeared in 1978.

It is in his poetry that by far his most valuable, individual contribution to literature lies. The critical study which follows will concentrate on the poetry, and above all the poetry in Scots (that is, the language of Lowland Scotland, "Lallans," as distinct from Gaelic: what is also sometimes referred to as "the Doric" or simply "the Vernacular"). There are three main reasons for giving most attention to his poetry in Scots. His best work is, I believe, in that language. It has had a deep influence, not only in stimulating work of high quality by other writers, but also in altering the whole literary and educational context in which Scots exists. And the third reason is this. If one asks why his work is not better known, especially in England, by far the commonest answer rests on the reputed difficulty of the Scots language. If this book can do anything to persuade readers beyond that sticking-point to take the poetry on its merits, it will be doing something useful.

Often enough, the English-speakers (including many Scotsmen) who report having most difficulty in understanding Scots are the same people who treat it dismissively as a mere dialect of English—not sufficiently different to merit consideration as a distinct language—and therefore, one would have thought, not so difficult as to be beyond their comprehension. In point of fact, the statement "Scots is a dialect of English" is only as true as the statement "English is a dialect of English." Which doesn't take us very far. But there is no need for an excursion into historical philology here. The fact most needful to bear in mind is simply that, prior to events resulting in the Union of 1603 (complemented by that of 1707), Scots played its due part among the national languages of Europe, with a healthy literature to show for it; and any changes thereafter were not due to some inherent disability in Scots as a language but to political or politico-religious decisions concerning its future.

Let an Englishman imagine for a moment a change round in that political situation, so that it was Scotland which was much the more powerful of the two kingdoms, and a Scots translation of the Bible had been eagerly received in England. The procedure which would then follow would be, not the uniting of Scotland to England (as James VI described the historical process), but the uniting of England to Scotland (an alternative of which he was well aware), with of course the language of the Predominant Partner, Scotland, being adopted for the United Kingdom. Let him then consider the thin dialect to which his English speech would inevitably be reduced, in comparison with the standard Scots which he would learn at school (where literature in English would scarcely get a mention) and which he would read constantly and endeavour, more or less, to speak. And finally, let him imagine with what feelings he might then look through the neglected volumes of some Etymological Dictionary of the English Language, or discover the equally neglected poets who wrote in that language before the Union.

That exercise may be useful presently, when one comes to the matter of how even a game with old words in a dictionary could alter literary history. But the starting-point now has to be Grieve's English rather than MacDiarmid's Scots. His early verse, like his prose, was written in English as a matter of course: there appeared to be no real alternative for a writer of any ambition in twentieth-century Scotland, and he certainly had no lack of ambition. English was also, of course, the language of the vast majority of the poems which he anthologised in three volumes as evidence of a literary revival in Scotland shortly after the first World War: a literary "Renaissance" in the sense in which people had been using the word about Irish writing. That was the situation when he first made his own mark as a poet, as the most accomplished of the younger members of the "Renaissance" group, writing in English.

REFERENCES

1. "Aims and Opinions," B.B.C. Third Programme, 9 Mar. 1960.
2. H. D. Harben, *The Rural Problem*, London 1913, p. vi.
3. *L.P.*, pp. 79, xv.
4. Letter to G. Thorburn, 14/5/27, in *Selected Letters of Edwin Muir*, ed. P. Butter, London 1974, p. 64.

CHAPTER II

PARNASSUS AND SCHIEHALLION

"Parnassus and Schiehallion are one."
("Valedictory," 1207.)

C. M. Grieve had established a considerable reputation
for himself as a poet writing in English before ever Hugh
MacDiarmid appeared on the scene, and though his early
English poems may now seem dated and of marginal
importance on the whole, some of them are still of considerable interest.

It is a mistake to suppose, as some commentators have
done, that because he modelled his three anthologies of
contemporary Scottish verse, *Northern Numbers*
(1920–1–2), on Edward Marsh's *Georgian Poetry* series, he
was himself an imitator of the English Georgians in terms
of style. In actual fact, where a specific influence is
discernible, it is likely to come, not from an English poet,
but from a European—Grieve keeping himself informed of
a wide range of recent European poetry, at any rate in
translation, as he was to demonstrate in many articles
(under various pseudonyms) in the *New Age*. And even a
poem such as his "Cattle Show," which might tend on the
face of it to recall the Georgian "country week-end" type
of production, is really something quite different:

> I shall go among red faces and virile voices,
> See stylish sheep, with fine heads and
>   well-wooled,
> And great bulls mellow to the touch,
> Brood mares of marvellous approach, and geldings
> With sharp and flinty bones and silken hair.

And through th' enclosure draped in red and gold
I shall pass on to spheres more vivid yet
Where countesses' coque feathers gleam and glow
And, swathed in silks, the painted ladies are
Whose laughter plays like summer lightning
        there.   (462.)

There are several points worth noticing here: the effect of
the odd technical expression ("brood mares of marvellous
approach," "coque feathers"), suggesting an informed
precision of observation; the very unusual handling of
rhythm, apparently "free" to begin with, but dominated
by the iambic pentameter from the last line of the first
stanza to the end; the deceptively bland juxtaposition of
images—the pure-bred animals on show and on sale, the
fine-feathered human aristocrats also on show (and could
it be on sale too?); the hint, in the "summer lightning" at
the end, of a storm to come, which might have a political
implication for anyone picking up the class-conscious
specification of "countesses" a couple of lines before. If
Georgian, this poem is something of a Georgian land-
mine.

    The most ambitious of Grieve's early poems in English,
"A Moment in Eternity," first appeared in 1922. Its
author thought well enough of it to choose it as one of the
few poems accompanying his prose in *Annals of the Five
Senses* (1923), to use it again in *To Circumjack Cencrastus*
(1930), and to open the edited-down volume of *Collected
Poems* with it in 1962. The poem has been adversely
criticised on stylistic grounds, and rightly so with regard
to its diction, which incorporates too many late-romantic
poetical gems, culled from Grieve's reading. In other
respects, however, it is technically quite impressive, particularly in the cunning manipulation of recurrent sound-
patterns, together with images of leaves, light, wind,
flame, and the colours of certain flowers. The poem
explores a moment of mystical illumination which by its

nature is strictly inexpressible, though it can be suggested
in symbolist fashion, and the proper context here is the
European symbolist movement rather than anything in
specifically English literature. Indeed, the poem might
have been written to illustrate this statement of the poet's
function by Vladimir Solovyov, himself a poet and a
religious philosopher who exerted a crucial influence on
the Russian symbolists: "Every true poet must penetrate
to 'the native land of flame and word' so as to borrow from
it the archetypes of his creations and the inner enlighten-
ment called inspiration which enables us to find even in
our natural world colours and sounds for the embodiment
of ideal patterns."[1]

That is exactly what is attempted through the aural,
visual and at times synaesthetic imagery of "A Moment in
Eternity;" and in addition, the archetypal tree of light in
the poem represents Solovyov's conception of Sophia, the
Wisdom of God, which so deeply affected the finest of the
Russian symbolist poets, Alexander Blok, in whom Grieve
was especially interested:

> Ah, Light,
> That is God's inmost wish,
> His knowledge of Himself,
> Flame of creative judgment,
> God's interrogation of infinity,
> Searching the unsearchable,
> —Silent and steadfast tree
> Housing no birds of song . . . .
>
> *O Thou,*
> *Who art the wisdom of the God*
> *Whose ecstasies we are!*   (7–8.)

Because of Grieve's tendency to deck it out with some
pretty faded posies of romantic English poetic diction, "A
Moment in Eternity" may appear deceptively old-
fashioned, especially when set against some of the more

experimental prose pieces in *Annals of the Five Senses*.
However, of the six prose specimens, the most successfully
executed are the least ambitious: "Café Scene" and
"Sartoria". The first of these may be associated with the
fact that the author had suffered attacks of malaria; at all
events, it depicts a physical and mental condition similar
to that caused by a fever, and does so brilliantly. The other
is a sort of mosaic built up from items about dress,
especially female dress, which suggests that the women's
fashion pages were part of the author's voracious reading.
It also reveals the passion for specialised terms and
esoteric vocabularies that was to become more prominent
in his later poetry: "I left him at the Haymarket standing
in the centre of the pavement murmuring over and over
again, 'Nainsook Directoire knickers trimmed with Swiss
insertion'."

Another prose piece, "The Never-Yet-Explored," is a
formidable attempt at investigating feminine psychology,
spoiled by over-writing and by the clumsy way in which
the author's reading is foisted on to a character who is
supposed to be the centre of attention in her own right.
This is indicative of a fault that also spoils "Cerebral."
Although the author's relationship with his subject-
matter is often intricately subtle, his relationship with the
reader can be startlingly naive. A reason for this may be
found in Grieve's "obscure but poignant sense of being an
entirely different person to himself." He is liable to stop
his narrative and point to this "entirely different person,"
asking the reader if he ever saw anything remotely
approaching *that* before, and forgetting that from the
reader's angle he is simply pointing at himself. Whatever
may be said in mitigation of this procedure, which is
recurrent in his work, it too often has the effect of throwing
the work out of perspective and irritating or indeed
antagonising the reader.

It is difficult to classify these prose pieces or briefly to
describe them. Grieve himself refers to them as "these psy-

chological studies, essays, mosaics (call them what you will) which I have (perhaps the best word in the meantime is) 'designed'."[2] Presumably he prefers the term "designed" to "written" because he is often working mosaic-fashion with materials quarried from the huge mass of reading stored away in his head or his notebooks. In the longest of these works, "A Four Years' Harvest," the method is at its weakest, and we are left looking back towards the quarries from which the various items came, instead of attending to the design which they are supposed to make.

Edwin Muir said when the *Annals* first appeared that the style struck him as being "in almost every way original and unusual."[3] But a great part of the impression of originality comes from the fact that Grieve is immensely more eclectic than anyone else. One cannot derive his style from particular sources because the sources are so many and so fantastically varied. This has obvious dangers, and Grieve speaks of his fear of having "paralysed his creative faculties by over-reading." What may have saved him from this in the end he describes as a "tiny specialist cell in his brain" which constantly experimented with an "obscure ray . . . emanating from his subtle realisation that beyond the individual mind of each man was a collective mind . . . The little specialist was able to use this pretty much as a man uses electricity or radium. The consequence was that he was enabled . . . to trace the thin line of his own mentality through all the incalculable fabric of the thought of humanity. This gave him latitude and longitude on the oceans of speculation."[4] Sometimes! Often enough, at any rate, to give Muir "that impression which can only be produced by the entry of a new personality, a new potentiality, into literature."

Grieve at this time was evidently immersed in psychological interests, but it was the psychology of intellectual processes that mainly held his attention. He is like a man who carries around with him a fascinating specimen: his own brain, preserved in "a strong solution of books" and constantly impinged upon by the media of magazines and newspapers. He pays minute attention to the effects of this bombardment of the brain, reverberating within an almost limitless memory, and gives the reader a running commentary on his observations. When the bombardment is most violent, so is the style of the observer, who keeps throwing parenthesis after parenthesis into false-bottomed sentences. Of course the brain is also subjected to sense impressions, and these are reported as well, but the observer is most interested in particles of information, other people's observations, ideas, facts.

At the end of it all the reader, a little exhausted, may feel that he has been left with some extraordinarily interesting fragments, but to fit them into a total design is quite another matter. Yet, on reflection, one can see certain patterns emerging from the *chaos décoratif*. One of these may be picked out by way of example:

He could not help wondering . . . whether intelligence itself was not an accident in the creative processes, or really the goal towards which mankind believed itself drifting|. . . He fell back on the old, old feeling that . . . if every opinion is equally insignificant in itself, humanity's bewilderment of thought is a mighty net which somehow holds the whole truth . . . .

So his tendency was always to the whole, to the totality, to the general balance of things. Indeed it was his chiefest difficulty (and an ever-increasing one that made him fear at times cancellation to nonentity) to exclude, to condemn, to say No. Here, probably, was the secret of the way in which he used to plunge into the full current of the most inconsistent movements, seeking, always in vain, until he was utterly exhausted . . . to find ground upon which he might stand four-square . . . .

He was always fighting for the absent, eager for forlorn hopes, a champion of the defeated cause, for those portions of truth which seemed to him neglected.[5]

One of these "forlorn hopes" he championed in a new periodical which he founded in the summer of 1922, the *Scottish Chapbook*. In his first editorial, he recalled a short-lived "Scots Renascence" which had centred around Patrick Geddes in Edinburgh and produced four numbers of a lavish periodical called the *Evergreen* in 1895–7. This had disappeared into the Celtic Twilight, and "the movement of which it was the organ scarcely outlasted it . . . . The Scottish literary revival proved to be a promise that could not be kept."[6] Clearly, Grieve intended to make, and keep, a bigger promise, and when Denis Saurat used the term "renaissance écossaise" about the *Scottish Chapbook* group he was only echoing Grieve himself, who in February 1923 avowed his belief in the possibility of "a great Scottish Literary Renaissance."[7] However, "Renaissance" is one of the big words that make us so unhappy, as Joyce put it, and the infant mortality rate of the new movement was high.

Grieve did his best to swell the ranks by becoming two people, as William Sharp ("Fiona MacLeod") had done before him in the *Evergreen* and elsewhere, and indeed as an extraordinary number of modern Scottish writers have done. "Hugh MacDiarmid" made his debut in the first number of the *Scottish Chapbook*, and since Grieve adopted this name almost to the exclusion of his patronymic, it is as MacDiarmid that he will be referred to from now on. (He used several other pseudonyms as well, but that is by the way.)

The first piece of work attributed to MacDiarmid was not a poem in Scots, as has often been supposed, but a sketchily dramatised specimen of English prose called "Nisbet: An Interlude in Post-War Glasgow." It is of no great literary value, but has some biographical interest, and casts some light on a matter of importance in his later work: his conception of Russia's role in history. Tacitly paraphrasing Spengler to the effect that all forms of literary and intellectual expression were approaching a dead-end in Western Europe and America, Nisbet declares that "we must wait . . . for the new beginning which will come from a civilization other than ours." And Young, the Communist propagandist who plays Judas to Nisbet's Christ, tells him that "the renewal is coming, has begun to come, from Russia . . . . In Dostoevsky is to be found the first delineation of that new world." Judas or not, it is with Young that Nisbet goes off at the end of the sketch.

This theme was not taken up in MacDiarmid's poetry until *A Drunk Man Looks at the Thistle* appeared in 1926. In the meanwhile an event of great importance in Scottish literary history took place.

MacDiarmid in later life confessed to having known very little about literature in Scots when he opposed the foundation in 1920 of the Vernacular Circle of the London Burns Club, writing soon after that event that the Scots vernacular "is, and will remain . . . a backwater of the true river of Scottish national expression." By August 1922, however, active support of "the campaign of the Vernacular Circle . . . for the revival of the Doric" was included in the programme for his *Chapbook*—a programme which insisted on a "distinctly Scottish range of values" and aimed to "encourage and publish the work of contemporary Scottish poets and dramatists, whether in English, Gaelic or Braid Scots." In the September issue of the magazine, Rebecca West's Edinburgh novel, *The Judge*, was reviewed, and the following month there appeared a "Monologue in the Vernacular" entitled "Following Rebecca West in Edinburgh" by Hugh MacDiarmid. There are actually two voices in this "monologue," one of which comments admiringly in English on the use of Scots by the other. The theme is the

need for a Scottish James Joyce who would do for Edinburgh what *Ulysses* had just done (in February of that
year) for Dublin, and it is postulated that such a writer
would find in the old Scots vernacular the verbal compost
needed for his purposes.

What follows is a phenomenon familiar to readers of
MacDiarmid's later poetry: the subject of his writing is
the kind of writing he would like to be able to write and
hopes will eventually be written. It seems to have
originated in a habit MacDiarmid acquired in the course
of his training in journalism, a profession in which
developments are sometimes reported before they have
actually occurred. Not that it is only journalists who sub-
stitute the advance hand-out for the reality, but it is
MacDiarmid the literary journalist, I think, who offers us
the advance hand-out as a form of literature.

"Following Rebecca West In Glasgow" might be called
a hoax, but it is more the work of a journalist in a hurry
than of a deliberate hoaxer. One need not go further than
the first three letters of the alphabet in Jamieson's
Etymological Dictionary of the Scottish Language to find the
more unfamiliar part of the Scots vocabulary used by
MacDiarmid, and most of his quotations and references to
literary works in Scots are there as well. Hoaxers are more
careful about covering their tracks.

Nor is this simply a literary joke, any more than it was
simply what he called a "pastime" which at this time
produced his first poems in Scots as a result of his encounter with Sir James Wilson's book on *Lowland Scotch as
Spoken in the Lower Strathearn District of Perthshire*. MacDiarmid's sense of humour was daft enough in all conscience,
but what lies behind both these instances is a serious
matter to any poet: the literal-mindedness which takes
him to dictionaries and the like because that is where the
words are, and words are meat and drink to poets. All that
was new in MacDiarmid's case was the extension of his
natural bent as a connoisseur of words so as to take in the

Scots language, a depleted dialect of which he had of course spoken in his boyhood in Langholm.

He had good reason to be doubtful of the potential of that language for the making of poetry, in view of the quality of Scots verse since Burns, and for that matter the restricted linguistic resources that Burns himself was able to exploit, in comparison with those freely at the disposal of an earlier Scots poet such as Dunbar. But certain out-of-the-way Scots expressions in Wilson's book attracted MacDiarmid's interest, some of them so strongly that he responded by using them in two short poems, which were attributed in a newspaper article to an anonymous friend of C. M. Grieve.[9] One of these, "The Blaward and the Skelly," he rightly thought so little of that he never reprinted it until its inclusion in his *Complete Poems* (1978). The other, "The Watergaw," appeared as the work of Hugh MacDiarmid, along with the Scots prose piece just mentioned, in the *Scottish Chapbook*. Its distinctive quality was quickly recognised. For Denis Saurat in 1924—as for Iain Crichton Smith in 1967—it was an authentic masterpiece, and it has become probably the best-known and most-admired of all MacDiarmid's poems. Its ending, so open to imaginative interpretation, seems to me to be likewise open to criticism, but its historical priority alone would require it to be quoted here before any other poem:

> Ae weet forenicht i' the yow-trummle
> I saw yon antrin thing,
> A watergaw wi' its chitterin' licht
> Ayont the on-ding;
> An' I thocht o' the last wild look ye gied
> Afore ye deed!

forenicht – early evening
yow-trummle – cold spell in July after sheep-shearing
antrin – occasional, rare
watergaw – indistinct or fragmentary rainbow

chitterin' – trembling, shivering
ayont – beyond
on-ding – beating down (of rain)
gied – gave
deed – died

There was nae reek i' the laverock's hoose
That nicht—an' nane i' mine;
But I hae thocht o' that foolish licht
Ever sin' syne;
An' I think that mebbe at last I ken
What your look meant then.   (17.)

The author, in the person of C. M. Grieve, editor of the *Scottish Chapbook*, was able to comment on his own work immediately it appeared there, as follows:

Doric economy of expressiveness is impressively illustrated in the first four lines of Mr. MacDiarmid's poem. Translate them into English. That is the test. You will find that the shortest possible translation runs something like this: "One wet afternoon (or early evening) in the cold weather in July after the sheep-shearing I saw that rare thing—an indistinct rainbow, with its shivering light, above the heavily-falling rain."[10]

One might question the loose rendering of "ayont" ("beyond") as "above," and the rather unidiomatic use of "antrin," but there can be no doubt about the expressive economy of such a word as "yow-trummle." "Yow-trummle" (literally "ewe-tremble," because this late cold-spell makes the shorn sheep tremble) is a metaphor ready-made for the poet, and MacDiarmid puts it to work by linking the shivering of the sheep with the shivering light of the rainbow, as he links the unexpected cold spell in summer with the sudden chill brought by the advent of death. The latter is suggested by the absence of "reek" (smoke from the hearth, hence warmth) in the speaker's home, conveyed by an extension of the proverbial expres-

reek – smoke
laverock – lark

sin' syne – since then

sion, "there's nae reek i' the laverock's hoose the nicht" ("there's no smoke in the lark's house tonight"—said when the night is cold and stormy). It is not unusual for a proverbial saying to be metaphorical; what is surprising about this one is the stretch of imagination required to grasp it.

MacDiarmid found it, with the other unusual Scots expressions, in Wilson. Obviously there is no word-for-word equivalent for most of them in English, and they have other values for the poet in addition to compression and the unmatchable appeal of Scots sounds to a Scots ear. For example, "watergaw" does not denote "rainbow" but rather a fragmentary or indistinct kind of rainbow—a precise word for a hazy phenomenon—and it functions in the poem with a symbolic subtlety it is hard to imagine anyone achieving with the English word. How would one juxtapose a symbolic rainbow and the last look of a dying person without an effect of sentimentality or emotional blatancy? For the reader of English poetry, the word "rainbow" is coated with accretions from the several generations of romanticism since Wordsworth. But if "watergaw" is known to the reader at all, it has no set associations except perhaps for those which may attach themselves to a countryman's observation of the weather—in which case it is bad weather rather than good that may be expected.

This plays against the traditional associations of the rainbow with hope and with a Biblical covenant between man and God, as is brought out by the speaker calling the light "foolish," which is felt in turn to reflect on the "last wild look" of the dying person. In Grieve's commentary on MacDiarmid's poem, he claimed that it was "disfigured by none of the usual sentimentality" found in post-Burnsian Scots verse, and added: "It has a distinctively Scottish *sinisterness* for which expression is too seldom found nowadays." This is of course information from outside the poem itself, but, provided one remains clear in one's mind about that point, there is no reason why criticism should not avail itself of any such material as proves useful to it. Likewise outwith the poem are indications that the dying person was the poet's father, turning to look at photographs of his two sons before he died. MacDiarmid himself repulsed any attempts to pursue these hints by saying that the poem was about "*anyone's* death." But he also assured at least one enquirer that the person who died was a man.[11] What makes the question of his identity worth bothering about is the psychological interest accruing to the circumstances if, when he turned to Scots, his first poem released his feelings about the death of his deeply religious father, which had come without warning at a time when the eighteen-year-old son was asserting his right to lead his life according to his own lights. And there is good reason to suspect that this was indeed the case.[12]

Although the poem shows, right from the start, MacDiarmid's sureness of touch and feeling for rhythm when he turned to writing verse in Scots, the vocabulary of "The Watergaw" inevitably raises a hoary question about which people tend to hold dogmatic views: the question of whether it is "proper" or "legitimate" for a poet to go looking for out-of-the-way, obsolescent or obsolete words which he then uses in a poem. With MacDiarmid, in certain cases, it is crucial that the reader should suspend judgment on that theoretical level and find his answer rather to the question of what this particular poet, with his particular talents, did with specific words in specific poems. There is, of course, a respectable enough theoretical argument, promoted energetically by MacDiarmid himself, for the revival of a neglected and fragmented language like Scots through a synthesis of its lexical resources which freely crosses historical and geographical lines of demarcation. Even Burns's usage is to some extent based on such a synthesis. But Burns is popularly regarded as a model of naturalness, at the furthest remove from a poet who would construct poems around assorted chance finds, picked up in some lexicographical backyard. A great deal obviously depends on what the reader has decided in advance to be "natural" and what "artificial" in verbal creative activity. MacDiarmid's practice was to approach Scots words, *any* Scots words, as potential material for poetry, and rely on his sensitivity to verbal stimuli to select what he could put to use imaginatively in a poem. And a competent reader of the poem must have sufficient good will to judge it on the basis of whether the poet put that material to good use in the given case.

Even the difficulty caused by unfamiliar words is not in any necessary sense a bad thing for the reader of poetry. By their very unfamiliarity, they sharpen our perception of verbal qualities to which we habitually pay too little attention, and invite a more positive response from our imaginations. The crux of the matter is then what the poet can offer our tuned-up faculties, other than just Rossetti's "stunning words for poetry."

But the verbal difficulty in MacDiarmid's Scots poems —certain deliberate *tours de force* apart—is not great. Relatively few of his best poems contain very out-of-the-way Scots expressions, and in any case the verbal tact with which he deploys them there is of the highest order. Many other poems scarcely go beyond the sparse Scots vocabulary of general modern usage or the colloquial range of what one would take to be his own childhood speech. No one willing to read Scots at all could have much difficulty with this, for example:

Empty Vessel

I met ayont the cairney
A lass wi' tousie hair
Singin' till a bairnie
That was nae langer there.

cairney – small heap of stones   tousie – tousled

Wunds wi' warlds to swing
Dinna sing sae sweet,
The licht that bends owre a'thing
Is less ta'en up wi't.   (66.)

The language here is very close to actual colloquial
speech in a country setting, ending with an idiom, *ta'en up
wi't*, which combines the idea of being engrossed in something with a suggestion of intimacy, used to startling effect
when applied to the light that bends over everything in the
universe. Any allusion of which the reader may be aware is
not literary but rather an echo of folk song. The first
stanza uses phrases from "Jenny Nettles," an old song
found at least as early as Allan Ramsay's *Tea-table
Miscellany* (1724–9), which shows by contrast the delicacy
of MacDiarmid's rhythmical sense. His verse-technique
looks conventional enough here, but it is made to do a lot
of work in a tiny space. Notice how the abrupt change in
focus from the country lass of the first stanza, with its
familiar Scots diminutives, to the cosmic worlds of the
second, is accompanied by an emphatic change in the
rhythmical pattern, enforced by alliteration and the
rhetorical emphasis of the negative, together with an
internal rhyme. Also impressive is the distillation into
eight short lines of those elements in the traditional
ballads that appealed to MacDiarmid most powerfully:
the stark treatment of mystery or tragedy; the sparse
detail that is specific without being explicit—only the
tousled hair by way of description of the girl or her
feelings, only the little cairn to suggest why her child is no
longer there; the switch without transition from the
natural to the more-than-natural; the defiant acceptance
of suffering as the distinction as well as the inevitable condition of human life. In the end, this tiny, simple-seeming

wunds – winds   a'thing – everything
dinna – don't   wi't – with it
owre – over

lyric encompasses in one gesture the light that bends over
all creation, the winds that swing the cosmic worlds, and a
mother singing to her dead child as though to rock it
asleep. And it affirms that the essentially human consciousness of love and suffering is at the heart of the
matter, the moral centre of the universe.

   Somewhat similarly, the little poem called "The Bonnie
Broukit Bairn" starts from a fragment of an old folk song
("The Bonnie Brucket Lassie"—it is by no means just
words one finds in Jamieson), and ends with the claim that
the depth of human suffering is such that the tears of the
Earth will drown the planets. Our Earth is seen as a
grubby, neglected but bonnie child, the music of the
spheres is reduced to idle gossip, and the language for
MacDiarmid's cosmic conceit is again close to colloquial
Scots. The meaning of *crammasy* ("crimson"), if not
already known from a much-anthologised ballad, might
be gathered from the French, and the context of *the haill
clanjamfrie* ("the whole jingbang") makes its meaning
clear enough:

> Mars is braw in crammasy,
> Venus in a green silk goun,
> The auld mune shak's her gowden feathers,
> Their starry talk's a wheen o' blethers,
> Nane for thee a thochtie sparin',
> Earth, thou bonnie broukit bairn!
> *—But greet, an' in your tears ye'll droun*
> *The haill clanjamfrie!*   (17.)

In its own way, this little poem supports an image of the
order of Shakespeare's

braw – handsome, grand
crammasy – crimson
mune – moon
gowden – golden
wheen o' blethers – pack of
   nonsense

broukit – streaked with dirt
   or tears, neglected
greet – weep
haill – whole
clanjamfrie – jing-bang

Pity, like a naked new-born babe,
Striding the blast, . . .
That tears shall drown the wind.

The form may look like a traditional stanza, but closer
inspection reveals MacDiarmid's practice of varying such
forms with individual touches which have quite subtle
effects. His forms are sometimes organic, in the sense that
he didn't know what form he was writing in until he
produced it, although of course in these early lyrics he was
committed in advance to the use of rhyme and a metrical
base as such—rather like Donne in the *Songs and Sonnets*.
The result in this case is the long-delayed rhyme between
lines two and seven, and the even longer wait before
crammasy at the beginning is part-rhymed with *clanjamfrie*
at the end.

As he rapidly found his own voice in Scots, however,
MacDiarmid showed a remarkable ability to give even
strictly conventional forms an individual stamp which
became quite unmistakable. In "The Innumerable
Christ," for example, he employs an almost too regular
metrical pattern, traditional imagery (even though
slanted in a less familiar direction), and an unexceptional,
simple Scots not unmixed with English. But the result is
somehow all his own work. His Scots verse is "more
simple, sensuous, and passionate" than anything he had
written in English, partly because the very act of writing in
Scots was an act of faith that heightened emotional commitment and clarified perspective, and partly because it
disencumbered his mind of echoes of all but a very few
other poets. He had much less to forget, and he had fewer
second thoughts, because from the start he had to entrust
more to feeling:

Wha kens on whatna Bethlehems
Earth twinkles like a star the nicht,
An' whatna shepherds lift their heids
    In its unearthly licht?

kens – knows   whatna – what kind of   the nicht – tonight

'Yont a' the stars oor een can see
An' farther than their lichts can fly,
I' mony an unco warl' the nicht
    The fatefu' bairnies cry.

I' mony an unco warl' the nicht
The lift gaes black as pitch at noon,
An' sideways on their chests the heids
    O' endless Christs roll doon.

An' when the earth's as cauld's the mune
An' a' its folk are lang syne deid,
On coontless stars the Babe maun cry
    An' the Crucified maun bleed.   (32.)

This poem was based on a speculation by the scientist
James Y. Simpson to the effect that "other worlds may
know their Bethlehems, and their Calvary too." MacDiarmid saw similarities between Simpson's evolutionary
theology and Solovyov's, and he seems to have in mind
here Solovyov's conception of the ultimate spiritualisation
of the cosmos in fulfilment of Christ's mission. Like Yeats,
MacDiarmid felt the need to construct in his poetry something to fill the void left by the destruction of a received
faith, and he was attracted to religious ideas not just on
the mythological but rather more on the theological—that
is, the intellectual—level. Like many declared atheists, he
was forever talking about God, whom he could not forgive
for failing to exist, and it is characteristic of several of his
finest early poems that, small as they are, they tend to
raise big questions to which religious answers are available.

    That seems to me to be the case with perhaps the finest
of them all, "The Eemis Stane", though it is certainly not

'yont – beyond   lift – sky
een – eyes   lang syne – long since
unco – strange   maun – must
warl' – world

incumbent upon the reader to consider religious implications there. The poem works by rendering an image so memorably that it stays with the reader and nags him into interpreting it imaginatively in his own fashion, perhaps long afterwards. New readers should perhaps be warned in advance that this is one of the constructions that make use of dictionary Scots, its opening line having been taken from an illustrative quotation in Jamieson. But the difficulty of this has been much exaggerated. A poet who himself wrote in Scots, Alexander Gray, declared of the expression *how-dumb-deid* that "for all I know, of my own knowledge, it may be a medicinal plant or a deep-sea fish, or one of the diseases of women."[13] And this despite the fact that if *how* had been spelt *howe* (a hollow), he would have been obliged to concede that all three component parts of the word were crystal-clear to him. But the crowning irony of his remark emerged when, in a book published a few years later, Gray himself used the word without seeing any need to include it in his glossary of Scots expressions.[14]

At least as important to the poem as the denotation of *how-dumb-deid* is its sound, with its three strong stresses balanced against *cauld hairst nicht* in the highly evocative, drawn-out opening line. And sound is obviously being exploited also in the phrase *like a yowdendrift*, used musically with first a falling and then a rising intonation:

I' the how-dumb-deid o' the cauld hairst nicht
The warl' like an eemis stane
Wags i' the lift;
An' my eerie memories fa'
Like a yowdendrift.

how-dumb-deid – silent dead (of night)	wags – shakes
hairst – harvest	yowdendrift – snow driven by the wind
eemis – unsteady	

Like a yowdendrift so's I couldna read
The words cut oot i' the stane
Had the fug o' fame
An' history's hazelraw
No' yirdit thaim.   (27.)

The Earth drifts through space like a stone, a dead star,
obscured by the uneasy memories of the speaker, falling
like snow driven by the wind, so that he couldn't read the
words on the stone, even if the moss of fame (in the old
sense of "rumour," "popular report") and the lichens of
history had not buried them. As I see it, the Earth has
become a tombstone marking the demise of its own life-
process, of which the only vestiges remaining are the moss
and lichens. The speaker is God, with His memories of
what He had hoped might come of life on Earth—an
interpretation for which there is support in other early
poems, most notably "The Dying Earth." The words
inscribed on the stone are signs of the Logos, which His
creature, Man, has failed to comprehend, and finally
obliterated in the course of human history.

One of the interesting aspects of "The Eemis Stane" is
the way in which it may be taken to illustrate the limitations of MacDiarmid's account of the process by which he
wrote the best of these poems: "The act of poetry [is] the
reverse of what it is usually thought to be; not an idea
gradually shaping itself in words, but deriving entirely
from words—and it was in fact . . . in this way that I wrote
all the best of my Scots poems."[15] In the light of that statement, consider this "epigram" by Grieve which appeared
in the *Scottish Chapbook* three months before MacDiarmid's
"Eemis Stane" was printed there:

Four wreaths a year old Time brings still
—No other mourner visiteth

fug – moss   yirdit – buried
hazelraw – lichen   thaim – them

This lonely stone of Earth that marks
The resting-place of Life and Death.[16]

The seasons are wreaths left by Time on the gravestone
which is the Earth—basically the same idea as appears in
"The Eemis Stane." And although it would no doubt be
inaccurate to talk about an idea gradually shaping itself in
words, is it not the case that there was an idea (or image)
which preceded the words of the Scots poem and was subsequently shaped by them?

MacDiarmid's account of the idea "deriving entirely
from words," which he supported by reference to
Mallarmé, was an over-simplification of the poetic
process, deliberately designed to be provocative, as so
many of his statements were. But there can be no doubt
that the impulse resulting in the writing of some of his
poems was generated by specific Scots words. In the case
of "Ex Vermibus," for example, a traditional rhyme
which he found in George Watson's *Roxburghshire Word-
Book* supplied the opening lines, and the rest of the poem
drew its imagery directly from Scots musical terms also in
Watson. The end-product is an analogy for the creative
relationship between MacDiarmid and the composer F.
G. Scott, whom he supplied with the words for many of his
finest songs, as he says in the poem he will supply the
song-bird with choice worms.

The importance of Scots *sounds* to MacDiarmid's own
creative process may be illustrated by another of his finds
in Watson: a linguistic example which had fascinated
several language specialists since Sir James Murray,
editor of the *Oxford English Dictionary*, first produced it.
Murray observed that Scots had retained the "guttural"
sound in words such as *eneuch* ("enough") which English
had lost, and that, furthermore, his own dialect of Upper
Teviotdale was distinguished by not one but three forms of
that fricative, used in accordance with the preceding
vowel, which they modified. He illustrated the use of the

labialised form, in particular, by the following example: *They're teuch sauchs growin' i' the Reuch Heuch Hauch* ("There are tough willows growing in the Reugh Heugh Haugh"—a meadow near Hawick). This specimen reappeared in Watson, and was duly transplanted into MacDiarmid's poem, "The Sauchs in the Reuch Heuch Hauch." It was not in the outcome a successful poem—the linguistic material was too much of a tongue-twister to start with—but it shows how the poet's imagination responded to the sounds as well as the vocabulary of Scots.

It would be hard to say whether MacDiarmid's most valuable contribution to Scots verse came from his eye or his ear. His ear was the subtler of the two, but Scots verse stood in most need of an eye for fresh imagery. Already in a few of his early English poems—most effectively perhaps in "Science and Poetry"—one is aware of what might be called a cosmological or cosmogonical eye, presenting in effect a God's-eye view of the universe; and this becomes deeply characteristic of a good deal of the imagery in his Scots poems. Its impact must have been much more novel in the Twenties than it is today, when space exploration has accustomed people to seeing on their television screens what MacDiarmid imaged in his imagination, but one comes across examples of something similar in Russian and German poetry of the earlier period. MacDiarmid kept himself well informed of such developments—as, on the other hand, of modernist experiments with "sound poetry," invented words, specialised vocabularies, dialect and non-standard usages of all sorts. His cosmological eye was brought into sharper focus through his use of Scots words—words which most commonly identify natural phenomena in a country setting—and the result of this, together with a compressed, sometimes laconic or sarcastic turn of phrase, is his own brand of Imagism. Indeed, one could use such poems in exemplary fashion to illustrate the technique of concentrating on the single image, or visual juxtaposition, and the associated Imagist principles of observing a drastic economy in the use of words, which should have hard, clear, dry qualities in order to avoid "emotional slither."

It is too fine a question to determine which of the elements to take first in his characteristic kind of imagery, which combines an eye for the cosmic with the countrified, blunt-spoken quality, of the earth earthy, traditionally associated with Scots speech. Consider the following passage of Scots prose, in which he begins by recalling the names of the various marbles he used to play with as a boy, and goes on to say that it is particularly when he becomes aware of the cosmos that the words are conjured up again:

> Glessies as bricht as Jenny's een, wi' coloured twirls
> inside them, and white cheeny anes, and green anes oot
> o' the taps o' lemonade bottles. Clay-davies, doolies,
> hard-hacks, mavies, cracksie-pigs, cullies—I'd a' the
> kinds. I mind o' them every time I see the stars reelin',
> and I can hardly look at a picter o' the globe—aye, or at
> the earth itsel' for the maitter o' that, as you whiles see
> it, no' in a toon, whaur it's a' crancrums and stour, but
> frae a braw brae tap, when you seem to see the haill o't
> birlin' clear as a penny afore you—without wantin' to
> cry "Holie for Nags!"[17]

From this point of view, the fantastic, sometimes grotesque ingredient in MacDiarmid's imagery, and especially in his cosmic high jinks, may be seen as the most natural of things, for its associations are with childhood, with the marvels of bairn sang—where the cow jumps over the moon just like that—and the imaginative lore of the folk. There certainly seems to be a connection between the quoted passage about boyhood games and the fantastic

glessies – glass marbles	crancrums – confused things
cheeny – china	stour – dust, commotion
mind o' – remember	birlin' – spinning
whiles – sometimes	

cosmic imagery—which is nonetheless clear, hard, and
objectively, often dramatically, presented—of such poems
as the "suite" called "Au Clair de la Lune," in which the
earth is a spinning top or a stone, while the moon is a
disreputable "craw o' a body" sitting on the four cross-
winds, or a piper, or a huntress with the oceans for her
dogs. The same is true of "Morning," in which the sun is
plunked in the sky like a frog in a cream-basin; "Krang,"
where the earth is the hulk of a whale whose bleached
bones are taken by the wind for a harp; and "Somer-
sault," in which West and East on the spinning world
become "the pigs at Gadara" and "a sow at the farrow."

These cosmic conceits have a primitive quality about
them that accords unobtrusively with his early interest in
Jung and the idea of a collective unconscious of the race.
He views them in

> the light that breaks
> From the whole earth seen as a star again
> In the general life of man.   (406.)

And it was a great advantage for him to be able to express
such a view in words that were clean and fresh rather than
smudged and worn, if only because they had been little
used for literary purposes in recent Scots history. The
raucle-tongued, earthy quality of Scots, already
mentioned, also ensured that the cosmic view would not
dissolve into the air-fairy. When the words are of a kind
associated in his mind with childhood, we get, not sentimentality or whimsy, but sheer devilment:

> Men see their warld turned tapsalteerie,
> Drookit in a licht owre eerie,
> Or sent birlin' like a peerie—
> Syne it turns a' they've kent till then
> To shapes they can nae langer ken.   (143.)

tapsalteerie – head-over-heels
drookit – drenched

owre – too
birlin' – spinning
peerie – top

Another gain for MacDiarmid came from the replace-
ment of the heated and at times embarrassingly self-
conscious eroticism of some of his earlier English poems
with a sort of grim frankness about sexual matters
reminiscent of the ballads, and in one of the Scots poems,
"Scunner," in particular, developed with considerable
psychological subtlety into an analysis of what from one
angle disgusts but from another excites the lover—strong
stuff for its time and place. It is a profound psychological
fact that, for Scotsmen, Scots is a much more virile
language than English, and MacDiarmid learned a tough,
masculine terseness of style from the Scots ballads, along
with their frankness.

There is also in his Scots poems a delight in the life of
animals, and in the grotesque; a familiarity with God
which used to be the special preserve of Scottish ministers
(writers being sent to the Devil for congenial company);
and a kirkyard humour, specialising in the Resurrection,
that was a familiar part of popular tradition. We pass from
a bird's eye view ("Whip-the-World") to an animal's eye
view ("Farmer's Death") to an idiot's ("Jimsy") to a
God's ("In the Pantry") and so on. The variety tends to be
more in the changing points of view than in the situations,
which are sometimes merely verbal in conception, this
being the weak side of what is only MacDiarmid's
strength when he has the imaginative resources to give the
words sufficient work to do. Lexical serendipity, or a
happy knack with dictionaries, can take him only so far.

In his second collection of Scots poems, *Penny Wheep*
(1926), as compared with the first, *Sangschaw* (1925), he is
less concerned about the company his best poems keep,
and there are too many which were made to jump out of
the dictionary into the cosmos by essentially the same con-
juring trick. "Blind Man's Luck" is an example of what I
mean. In Jamieson's *Dictionary*, the expression "oon eggs"
(eggs laid without the shell; addled eggs) is illustrated by
a quotation from an historical drama on Mary Stuart: "O

how he turn'd up the whites o' his een, like twa oon eggs."
MacDiarmid's poem follows:

> He juist sits oolin' owre the fire
> An gin a body speak t' him, fegs,
> Turns up the whites o's een
> Like twa oon eggs.
>
> "I've riped the bike o' Heaven," quo' he,
> "And whaur ma sicht s'ud be I've stuck
> The toom doups o' the sun
> And mune, for luck!"   (46.)

MacDiarmid could do that sort of thing with such ease
that there was a danger of its becoming a formula.
However, he had the good sense to see this for himself, and
already in *Sangschaw*, in a longer poem called "The Ballad
of the Five Senses," he had begun to try something quite
different in Scots. This poem shows no particular concern
with the peculiarities of the Scots language, no special
emphasis on the vocabulary that distinguishes it from
southern English. Its usage is largely colloquial, involving
Scots forms, of course, but sometimes distinguished from
English by suggesting the written equivalent of thinking
with a Scots accent. Yet the subject-matter is such that
one feels anyone else would have written about it in highly
literary English—as indeed he himself had done in "A
Moment in Eternity"—for this poem deals with an
experience very similar to that. Despite its title, it is concerned with getting *beyond* the senses to "mystical"
experience, and it launches into metaphysical speculations about beings in the universe whose senses are as
different from ours as what we call life is from what we call
death. The distance in terms of style between this poem

oolin' – crouching   riped – ransacked
gin – if   bike – nest (of bees)
body – person   toom – empty
fegs – faith!   doups – bottoms

and "A Moment in Eternity" is vast, but it is the intensity of the same mind that is conveyed in both. Stylistically, the Scots is pared down: it sheds the adjectival layers of the English.

One of the unexpected things about the "Ballad of the Five Senses" is the use of the old ballad measure for such a metaphysical subject. Another is the subtle kinship between the poet revealed in it and the Donne of such poems as "A Nocturnal Upon St. Lucy's Day," in which use is made of definition by negatives and similes of difference instead of the customary likeness. Appropriately enough, it was in the "Ballad" that George Russell ("AE") found the lines which made him feel that MacDiarmid and he had been "born under the same star," though he said: "I soon found that the circle of our beings intersected only at that one point, and, instead of the attraction of affinities, I began to feel the attraction which opposites have for us."[18]

In *Penny Wheep*, along with the second batch of short lyrics in the style that had become so characteristic of MacDiarmid, he included three longer poems which made much more extensive use of native Scots resources than the "Ballad" had done in developing a medium for sustained thought. The linguistic medium he was gradually evolving is "synthetic" in the sense that it synthesises diverse elements from Scots dialects, from old and current Scots usage, and from English. It is a literary idiolect created by the poet for his own purposes, and controlled by his feeling for the Scots speech of his boyhood, his native tongue. The essential point about this language, for the poet and his readers, is as stated by David Daiches: "The proof of the pudding is in the eating, and the best language is that which *works*."[19]

The first of these longer poems, "Sea-Serpent," speculates on the possibility of the human mind attaining an awareness of the essence of life, the original unity running through all the multi-variety of its forms. Like

Solovyov, MacDiarmid makes imaginative use of Gnostic
beliefs about the Creation as a process emanating from the
original essence of Godhead, and the redemption of spirit
from matter by spiritual knowledge. One of the Gnostic
sects, the Ophites, worshipped the serpent as the embodiment of divine wisdom, and the poet puts their myth to
work in his poem. It builds up impressively to an invoca-
tion of the primal serpent encircling the world, the first
expression of life as it issued fresh from the mind of God, in
the most majestic lines heard in Scots verse for four
centuries. That long wait suggests why, in this language, a
modern poet could still work up such a head of steam from
the old rhetoric. The rest is a matter of talent:

> O Thou that we'd fain be ane wi' again
> Frae the weary lapses o' self set free,
> Be to oor lives as life is to Daith,
> And lift and licht us eternally.
> Frae the howe o' the sea to the heich o' the lift,
> To the licht as licht to the darkness is,
> Spring fresh and fair frae the spirit o' God
> Like the a'e first thocht that He kent was His.
>
> Loup again in His brain, O Nerve,
> Like a trumpet-stang,
> Lichtnin-clear as when first owre Chaos
> Your shape you flang
> —And swee his mind till the mapamound,
> And meanin' o' ilka man,
> Brenn as then wi' the instant pooer
> O' an only plan!   (50–51.)

The second poem, "Bombinations of a Chimera," is a
set of variations based on "texts" somewhat similar to
Blake's "Proverbs of Hell." It is the process of thought,

howe – hollow   swee – sway
heich – height   brenn – burn
loup – leap

speculation along first one line, then another which may contradict the first, that matters in the poem, rather than any conclusions to be drawn from the arguments. Scots verse is here being intellectualised, and the appeal of the poetry is made from, and to, the dialectical movement of the mind: a rhythm of thinking.

The third of the longer pieces, "Gairmscoile," is very different. It is a poem not only *in* Scots but *about* Scots, and the title indicates that it is intended as a rallying-call to other poets to keep the language alive, like that sent out by the Irish poet John O'Twomey in 1754. It begins with a powerful evocation of the brute nature of man; passes from primitive sex to primitive language, these being seen as intimately linked; suggests that the key to "the spirit of the race" is to be found in the phonetic basis of language; encompasses several literary allusions, particularly to Wergeland, the champion of the *Landsmaal* movement in Norway, who was partly of Scots descent; and ends with a vitriolic flyting in the manner of Dunbar, insulting and castigating three unfortunate versifiers who apparently had indicated their disapproval of MacDiarmid's experiments with Scots. What he calls the "cast-offs" of the neglected and despised Scots vocabulary, which he is reviving as he writes the poem, are like animals of a species seemingly rejected and passed over in the evolutionary process. But now "Life hears beasts rowtin' that it deemed extinct." Potential for future development survives in the most primitive elements of the language:

> Mony's the auld hauf-human cry I ken
> Fa's like a revelation on the herts o' men
> As tho' the graves were split and the first man
> Grippit the latest wi' a freendly han'.
> . . . And there's forgotten shibboleths o' the
>   Scots
> Ha'e keys to senses lockit to us yet

> —Coorse words that shamble thro' oor minds like
>   stots,
> Syne turn on's muckle een wi' doonsin' emerauds
>   lit.   (73–4.)

There is here the essence both of J. M. Synge's view that
"before verse can be human again it must learn to be
brutal,"[20] and of Robert Frost's attempt to "write down
certain brute throat noises so that no one could miss them
in my sentences. I have counted on doubling the meaning
of my sentences with them."[21] But MacDiarmid went far
beyond this in claiming an imaginative empathy with the
Scots vernacular as

> a vast unutilised mass of lapsed observation made by
> minds whose attitude to experience and whose specula-
> tive and imaginative tendencies were quite different
> from any possible to Englishmen and Anglicised Scots
> today . . . We have lost (but may perhaps reacquire)
> word forming faculties peculiar to the Doric for the
> purposes of both psychological and nature description.
> There are words and phrases in the Vernacular which
> thrill me with a sense of having been produced as a
> result of mental processes entirely different from my
> own and much more powerful. They embody observa-
> tions of a kind which the modern mind makes with
> increasing difficulty and weakened effect.[22]

But what are the "shibboleths o' the Scots" which he
said "ha'e keys to senses lockit to us yet"? A shibboleth is
a *sound* that can be used in a password, and the poet
declares, in a passage in "Gairmscoile" which he italicises
for the reader's benefit:

stots – bullocks   emerauds – emeralds
doonsin' – dazzling

It's soon', no' sense, that faddoms the herts
  o' men,
And by my sangs the rouch auld Scots I ken
E'en herts that ha'e nae Scots 'll dirl richt
  thro'
As nocht else could—for here's a language
  rings
Wi' datchie sesames, and names for nameless
  things.   (74.)

In this key-passage he has the words act out the meaning.
In *dirl, rouch, richt, nocht*, his language does have sounds
which English lacks with which to fathom the hearts of
men. Scots was for him "a quarry of subtle and significant
sound."[23] And sound was the crux of his *gairmscoile*, his
call to the "school" of Scots poets he hoped to rally to the
old language—as in fact, in time, they did—because, he
said:

> I have a feeling that the meanings of words are of far less
> consequence than their sounds; that their total effects,
> physical and intellectual, are of infintely greater impor-
> tance than their purpose as media of rational expres-
> sion. . . . There are certain old Scots words which
> (apart altogether from their precise original significa-
> tion) have a significance of sound and shape which may
> prove infinitely suggestive. . . . I think that if Scottish
> artists will hunt out all these old words, the mere shapes
> and sounds of them will suggest to them effects which
> they cannot at present contrive, and if they set to and
> secure these effects the results will constitute a Scottish
> idiom—a Scottish scale of sound-values and physico-
> psychical effects completely at variance with those of
> England.[24]

I have quoted, along with the lines from "Gairmscoile,"

soon' – sound   nocht – nothing
rouch – rough   datchie – cunning, secret
dirl – thrill

passages from the prose in which MacDiarmid worked at a "theory of Scots letters" to back up the poems he was writing. The theory is not necessary for the poems, but it can clarify aspects of his thinking about them. The language issue was central to him, and it was psychologically based: "From this point of view, the value of the Doric lies in the extent to which it contains lapsed or unrealised qualities which correspond to 'unconscious' elements of distinctively Scottish psychology." And he believed that his "rouch auld Scots" could free him from restrictions which he felt had been built into literary English. "The genius of the English language now exercises an automatic moral censorship." But James Joyce had recently shown one way of breaking its shackles, and: "We have been enormously struck by the resemblance—the moral resemblance—between Jamieson's *Etymological Dictionary of the Scottish Language* and James Joyce's *Ulysses*. A *vis comica* that has not yet been liberated lies bound by desuetude and misappreciation in the recesses of the Doric: and its potential uprising would be no less prodigious, uncontrollable, and utterly at variance with conventional morality than was Joyce's tremendous outpouring."[25]

The Irishman Joyce was the most European of writers in English. And throughout Europe there had recently been more or less radical attempts at revitalising the linguistic resources of literature, including revivals of languages long neglected. In matters of technique, MacDiarmid claimed that he had found in Scots a unique, unexploited potential for "the very effects and swift transitions which other literatures are for the most part unsuccessfully endeavouring to cultivate." He was now ready to try his hand at a really big poem in Scots: a major work with which he would stake Scotland's national claim to make a contribution to the literature of Europe, as she had done in the past. This work was *A Drunk Man looks at the Thistle*, which calls for another chapter.

REFERENCES

1. A *Solovyov Anthology*, ed. S.L. Frank, London 1950, p. 39.
2. *A.,* Dedication "To John Buchan."
3. "Readers and Writers,"*N.A.,* 15 Nov. 1923, pp. 32–3.
4. *A.,* p. 19.
5. *A.,* pp. 15, 194–5.
6. *S.C.,* Aug. 1922, p. 4.
7. "Le Groupe de 'La Renaissance écossaise'," *R.A.,* Apr. 1924. *S.C.,* Feb. 1923, p. 182.
8. *S.C.,* Aug. & Sep. 1922, pp. 15–19, 46–50.
9. *Dunfermline Press,* 30 Sep. 1922, p. 7. (First noted by D. Glen, *Hugh MacDiarmid and the Scottish Renaissance,* Edinburgh 1964, p. 75.)
10. "Causerie," *S.C.,* Oct. 1922, pp. 62–3.
11. J. Kocmanová, "Art and Revolution in the Poetry of Hugh MacDiarmid," *Philologica Pragensia,* 5 (1962), p. 222.
12. See K. Buthlay, "The Appreciation of the Golden Lyric," *SLJ,* July 1975, pp. 41–66.
13. "Lallans: a Plea for the Kailyaird," *Burns Chronicle,* 1950, p. 11.
14. *Four-and-Forty,* Edinburgh 1954, p. xxv.
15. *L.P.,* London 1943, p. xiii.
16. *S.C.,* Dec. 1922, p. 122.
17. "Holie for Nags," *S.O.,* 22 Sep. 1928, p. 5.
18. "Introductory Essay," *First Hymn to Lenin,* London 1931, p. 2.
19. "Introduction," *A Drunk Man Looks at the Thistle* (1953), p. xviii.
20. "Preface," *Poems and Translations,* Dublin 1912, pp. xi–xii.
21. Quoted by J. Isaacs, *Listener,* Apr. 1954, p. 566.
22. "A Theory of Scots Letters —II," *S.C.,* Mar, 1923, pp. 210–11.
23. *Ibid,* p. 210. MacDiarmid's use of Scots sounds is discussed in K. Buthlay, "Shibboleths of the Scots," *Akros,* Aug. 1977, pp. 23–47.
24. "Music: Braid Scots Suggestions," *Scottish Nation,* 5 June 1923, p. 14.
25. *S.C.,* Feb. 1922, p. 183.

CHAPTER III

DIVINE INEBRIETY

What is immediately impressive about *A Drunk Man Looks at the Thistle* (1926) is the range and variety which MacDiarmid encompasses in a single work. In various metrical forms, there are short lyrics, longer poems along similar lines to "Sea-Serpent," satires of contemporary Scotland, a political ballad, adaptations of modern European poets, grotesquely comic pieces, displays of "metaphysical" wit, and sustained flights to the most rarefied reaches of speculative thought. The protagonist struggles with a series of dilemmas in terms of his own nature and that of his country, mankind and the world, the cosmos and the Unknown God. This protagonist, the Drunk Man, is more and, in a strictly artistic sense, less than the poet. One is aware of him between the individual poems and often enough within the poems themselves, as if the rest of life were insisting on invading formal art, claiming a place in it. A modern technique, the "stream of consciousness," was newly available as a possible way of handling this, and MacDiarmid was enough of a modernist to make use of it. But the consciousness rendered in the poem is itself potentially creative, passing from memory to reflection, from sense-impressions to metaphysical speculations, and seeking to interpret to itself its own flux in terms of analogy and metaphor, symbol and myth.

Beyond the jagged line of consciousness with its often violent incongruities, there are threads of allusion which are spun out in the course of the poem to sustain its precarious sense of unity. Precarious, but sufficient for most knowledgeable critics of the work to regard this as MacDiarmid's masterpiece, one of the great poems of modern literature. True, a Marxist commentator has complained that "no-one has produced an account of what the latter two-thirds of the poem does in proportion to that blizzard of images of Man, thistle, and Eternity."[1] But what he seems to be asking is for some other critic to supply an interest in the poem's network of ideas which he lacks: ideas which in any case his own ideological bent would be unlikely to respond to. More than half a century after it was written, it is not so easy to pick up some of the allusions one needs in order to get one's bearings in the poem, particularly in the later stretches where MacDiarmid's head was full of literary, metaphysical and religious ideas with which not too many readers today are familiar. One has to persevere with this poem if one is to enjoy all it offers. But its rewards are very great.

The title, *A Drunk Man Looks at the Thistle*, suggested by F. G. Scott, has put many people off from the start. Some might concede that a certain literal-mindedness is necessary to the poet, as well as his sense of the figurative, but hardly to this extent. More than two and a half thousand lines of looking at the thistle? Well may the man confess to inebriation! Also, from a linguistic point of view, a French critic has objected that the title is unsuitably English for a work so thoroughly Scots. But "a drunk man" is in fact a Scottish idiom, with a usage that is quite sufficiently foreign to Southern English ears.

One might suspect that the trouble with the title is that it seems altogether too "Scotch," too redolent of the national obsession with strong liquor. However, Owen Dudley Edwards has suggested the influence of G. K. Chesterton's poem, "The Rolling English Road," a road allegedly made by the rolling English drunkard, of whom we are told that "the wild rose was above him when they found him in the ditch." It might have been a short step from that English rose to the Scots thistle, seen by the

Drunk Man in similar circumstances at the roadside. Certainly Chesterton—"or somebody else as famous if less
fat"—is observed satirically in MacDiarmid's poem, participating in the ritual of a Burns Supper, the height of
Scottish phoniness to the poet. But there is an interest
beyond the satire in what Chesterton actually said on just
such an occàsion, at the London Burns Club in 1923. He
said that the more narrowly national Burns was, the more
universal he became. He only failed when he took himself
seriously as an "English" poet and wrote in English. And
Chesterton went on to observe that "Scots are insulted
daily with all sorts of complaints of their shrewdness and
their stolidity. In the face of a hundred glorious examples
to the contrary they are told that they are sober; most
slanderous of all, they are accused of being law-abiding."
In actual fact, as their history and the strong strain of
revolt in their literature show, they are wild, violent, and
cruel to the point of vindictiveness, but also with a passion
for freedom. They are "more elevated, more mystical, and
more violent" than the English.[2]

Anyone reading, for example, the Drunk Man's
comment on his compatriots—"Nae doot they're sober, as
a Scot ne'er was"—will see the relevance of Chesterton's
remarks to a good deal more than the title of the poem.
And it is that sort of poem: scattered throughout with allusions that have unexpected but significant associations. It
is not possible to explore such allusiveness adequately
here, but it may be useful to plant a few sign-posts along
the way. For example, near the beginning of *A Drunk Man*,
there is an excellent version (via an English inter-
mediary[3]) of Alexander Blok's poem, "Neznakomka," in
which the Russian poet's need for the stimulation of drink,
and his ambiguous vision of the mystical Sophia now
transformed into a fashionable prostitute, link up with the
Drunk Man and his similarly ambiguous relationship
with his eternally feminine Muse. The associations are
then extended in another poem adapted from Blok, and

MacDiarmid would hope that a little more interest in this greatest of recent Russian poets might recall to the reader his lyrical drama of the same title, which opens in a pub from which the Poet is kicked out for getting too drunk. But the deeper significance of Blok's appearance in *A Drunk Man* (as will be seen from what follows below) is suggested by the key-notes of his later poetry—"one continuous dissonance between the Real and the Ideal" —and its kinship with Dostoevsky's "world of antithesis."[4]

Of course, the drunkenness of MacDiarmid's protagonist is symbolic: he says explicitly that it doesn't matter what gives us the lift we need—"The barley bree, ambition, love,/Or Guid or Evil workin' in's"—and he sees poets as no different from other men "save when genius mak's them drunk." But his actual tipple, whisky, is clearly symbolic too, being the now much adulterated and diluted national spirit. Likewise the thistle, the national emblem, growing in the bracken where he finds himself sprawling outside the pub, which is the "Gillha'" (glossed as "the hostelry of life"). Thistles are on the decline like everything else in Scotland in 1926, but there are specimens of special virtue still being cultivated in the poet's birthplace, Langholm: magnificent specimens, at least eight feet high, reared to play their part in the Border ritual of the Common Riding, which is celebrated in the poem itself as a genuine expression of the Scottish ethos, and described in more detail in MacDiarmid's Scots prose sketch, "The Common Riding."[5]

On a different level, extending the metaphysical dimension of the poem, the Drunk Man ponders the question of what gave the thistle its disturbing, inchoate shape. To his inflamed imagination it looks in the moonlight like a tortured body, sketchily improvised to hold a soul, but growing monstrously till it fills the whole universe, like

the barley bree – whisky

Yggdrasill, the tree that in Norse mythology holds all the worlds together, only to shrink again "like a reistit herrin'." The moon allows him to see the mystery of life embodied in the thistle in a different light from that of common day, but a much more ambiguous one. It lights the scene for the Drunk Man's monologue, in which individual poems are carried along on the stream of consciousness, liberated by the whisky, ebbing and flowing with the moon.

The setting of this dramatic monologue is suggestive of his national literary tradition, some of the props having been provided by Gregory Smith, who saw the distinctive features of the literature of the Scot in what he called the Caledonian Antisyzygy (combination of opposites):

> Does literature anywhere, of this small compass, show such a mixture of contraries as his in outlook, subject, and method, real life and romance, everyday fact and the supernatural, things holy and things profane, . . . thistles and thistledown? . . . The sudden jostling of contraries seems to preclude any relationship by literary suggestion. The one invades the other without warning. They are the "polar twins" of the Scottish Muse.

Smith says that this characteristically Scottish "conjunction of opposite moods" issues, in the words of Gavin Douglas, in "dremis or dotage in the monis cruick" (moon's crook). And he points out that Scots poets, with tongue in cheek, tend to explain this away as accountable to the national drinking habits—a tactic which is really

> a quizzing of those prosaic and precise persons who must have that realism which presents everything as sober fact, within an ell of their noses. The poets seem to say: "Here is a fantasy strange enough; if you, drunkard of facts, must explain it, do so in the only way open to you . . . . Be satisfied, if you think it is we who are drunk.

As for us, let the contrast be unexplained, and let us make merry in this clash of strange worlds and moods."[6]

This is picked up in the "Author's Note" to *A Drunk Man*, in which MacDiarmid defiantly describes the work as a "gallimaufry," and warns readers against attempting to confer "a species of intelligibility foreign to its nature upon my poem," since "drunkenness has a logic of its own."

Even so sympathetic a critic as William Soutar saw this as at best "a brilliant manoeuvre by which he shifts the onus of responsibility upon his readers;" and Soutar granted only a "semblance of consistency, . . . a consistency of emotional tone," to the work as a whole.[7] But it has much more than that. MacDiarmid makes structural use of his master-images of Thistle, Rose, Whisky and Moon in two ways, recharging them with such potential that they act as symbolic centres to which clusters of fresh images are attracted, or treating them as themes for sets of variations, in a flow of imaginative and fanciful invention unsurpassed by any modern poet.

Consider even a subsidiary image such as the sea-serpent from the poem in *Penny Wheep*, of which an elusive glimpse is caught early in *A Drunk Man*. It reappears as the world-serpent in the Yggdrasill myth already referred to, along with the dragon gnawing at the root of the cosmic tree, the branches of which drip honey on which bees feed; and the poet not only makes effective use of that string of images but also extends the associations of the sea-serpent in a cluster that includes the octopus and the white whale, Moby Dick. It will be useful perhaps to illustrate the latter point through his adaptation of another Russian poet, showing how MacDiarmid's general aim of restoring an international context for Scots poetry was made to contribute in very practical fashion to the structure of *A Drunk Man*. He took a poem by Zinaida Hippius called "Ona"

("She") in the Russian and "Psyche" in the English crib
he was using. The word "poulp" meaning an octopus was
introduced into the English version, and MacDiarmid
adopted "The Octopus" as his title when he supplied one
for this section of *A Drunk Man*. The degeneration of the
potent, primitive image of the sea-serpent, in the guilt-
ridden female sexuality of Hippius's poem, then passes
through the forms of flabby octopus and dozent dragon to
the final shock of recognition:

> And this deid thing, whale-white obscenity,
> This horror that I writhe in—is my soul!   (94.)

Compare the English version from which he was working:

> And this dead thing, this loathsome black impurity,
> This horror that I shrink from—is my soul.[8]

The octopus, the dragon, the serpent and the white
whale will each surface again for other purposes in *A
Drunk Man*. At this point, they all contribute on the psychological level to what the poet called the "psycho-
somatic quandary" of human sexuality, which he
explored in a long sequence with ultimately religious
implications, the effect of which in Scotland in 1926 has
been likened to "a childbirth in church."[9] The "psycho-
somatic quandary," like the sado-masochist theme in the
poem, is a modern version of the combination of opposites,
and the way in which MacDiarmid brings out its special
significance for him may be illustrated by another adaptation which now becomes part of the fabric of the work, this
time from Else Lasker-Schüler. The poem was called
"Sphinx," but it associated the sphinx with the moon, and
MacDiarmid for obvious reasons concentrated on the
moon image. He follows his English crib[10] closely for the
first five lines; then, jettisoning all the scented boudoir
imagery which follows in the original, he homes in on the
last line, "Finding their strength in conflict's tortured

dozent – impotent

hour," and transforms it into this:

> But ilka windin' has its coonter-pairt
> —The opposite 'thoot which it couldna be—
> In some wild kink or queer perversity
> O' this great thistle, green wi' jealousy,
> That breenges 'twixt the munelicht and my hert. (96.)

The thistle gives the Antisyzygy its Caledonian stamp.
In a basic sense, MacDiarmid's subject in *A Drunk Man* is
the writing of that work. He is very consciously a Scottish
poet, setting out to recreate the ethos of his people in a
major poem. The nature of that ethos has been preserved
in their literature, and, as he learned all too well from
Gregory Smith, its great distinguishing feature is the
Caledonian Antisyzygy. So the "routh o' contrairies"
subsumed under the thistle attests to the authenticity of
the poem.

But what if Gregory Smith were wrong? Well, not just
the Drunk Man but even so sober and respectable a
character as John Buchan (in his introduction to *The
Northern Muse*, 1924) believed otherwise, and the essential
validity of the Caledonian Antisyzygy has been accepted
by subsequent historians of Scottish literature such as
Kurt Wittig. But the question is not really important,
because, granted that some aspects of the phenomenon
may be particularly conspicuous in certain
literatures—and one of these would surely be the Russian
to which MacDiarmid was so attracted at this time—antisyzygy as such can be found in *any* literature. The reason
for this is that it is a function of the imagination, as can be
seen for example in Coleridge's account of that faculty in
terms of "the balance or reconciliation of opposite or
discordant qualities." To the extent that MacDiarmid
succeeded in expressing antisyzygy authentically in his
poem, therefore, he was carrying out his intention,

ilka – every   breenges – plunges
'thoot – without   routh – abundance

because to that extent he was producing a genuinely imaginative work of Scots literature.

However, it is significant that the idea of antisyzygy or *coincidentia oppositorum* is not in Coleridge's mind confined to aesthetics but becomes a fundamental philosophical principle informing the whole range of his later thinking. And as such it is by no means confined to Coleridge but is featured conspicuously in, for example, Blake, Schelling, and Hegel. It was a seminal idea long before, in the Neoplatonists and the occult tradition in general, and was to become the basic principle of Yeats's system in *A Vision* (1925), which MacDiarmid simultaneously decried and made us of.[11] Many forms of dynamic philosophy or religious thought issue in the principle of complementary tension between polar opposites, as between *yin* and *yang*, and there is no doubt that MacDiarmid was aware of some of the wider implications of the "polar twins."

One of the ways in which Coleridge expressed the idea of *coincidentia oppositorum* was through his favourite adage, 'extremes meet,' and this is paralleled by the Drunk Man when he adopts his characteristic philosophical stance early in the poem: "I'll ha'e nae hauf-way hoose, but aye be whaur/Extremes meet." (87.) However, as the reader reaches the later parts of the poem, it becomes clear that it is not of Coleridge he should be thinking but rather of Nietzsche and above all Dostoievsky, who said of himself "I always go to extremes; I have exceeded the limit all my life," and who had characters such as Alyosha and Mitya Karamazov declare that they "would admit of no half-way house," and that "God makes nothing but riddles . . . [where] extremes meet and all the contraries exist side by side."

In February 1926, when *A Drunk Man* was no more than a quarter of its length as published, it contained a section designed as "Homage to Dostoievsky"—one of the Russian writers in whom there was very lively interest in Britain at this time—and the published work shows the impact of that "appalling genius" in much more than the two sections directly addressed to him. This influence is clear enough when the Drunk Man speaks of the need to explore misery and madness, disease and death, and claims a special insight into the morbid depths of the mind; but there is a less familiar aspect of Dostoevsky which is important to the poem, though handled in such a way that readers may not so easily take the point. It is smuggled in by way of a sardonic joke about the Scots being, as Dostoievsky claimed for the Russians, *narodbogonosets* (a God-bearing people). Scottish pretensions in this respect have suffered in the abject national decline; nevertheless, as the Biblical stone which the builders rejected became the head-stone of the corner, so Scotland may yet discover her destiny "and yield the *vsechelovek*" (the Universal Man or Pan-Human).

His use of these Russian expressions (134) is a clear indication that MacDiarmid has been reading D. S. Mirsky's *Modern Russian Literature* (1925). And there it is noted that Dostoievsky's greatest triumph in his lifetime, and the fullest assertion of his nationalist faith, was the speech in 1880 in which he claimed that Pushkin, the national poet who could paradoxically identify himself with other nationalities, was the type of the Universal Man: "This Pan-Humanity is the national characteristic of Russia, and Russia's mission is to effect the final synthesis of all mankind."[12] Hence the Drunk Man's "whim (and mair than whim):"

> To seek the haund o' Russia as a freen'
> In workin' oot mankind's great synthesis.   (135.)

The suggestiveness of the allusion becomes more apparent if one is aware that Father Zossima in *The Brothers Karamazov* applies to Russia, despised by the West, the same Biblical analogy of the stone the builders

freen'—friend

rejected which the Drunk Man applies to "puir auld
Scotland." And MacDiarmid then proceeds to use
Dostoievsky's Russian Idea (the Idea which it is Russia's
destiny to contribute to history) in the culmination of the
long section addressed to the great Russian writer which
follows. This Idea—it demands a capital letter—involved
the reconciliation of Russia's own internal contradictions
as well as the conflicts between nations, and the poet aims
to play his part in it by constructing a unity from the
contrary qualities of *his* nation, thus achieving a resolution
of the Caledonian Antisyzygy:

> For a' that's Scottish is in me,
> As a' things Russian were in thee,
> And I in turn 'ud be an action
> To pit in a concrete abstraction
> My country's contrair qualities,
> And mak' a unity o' these
> Till my love owre its history dwells,
> As owretone to a peal o' bells.   (145.)[13]

The Russian Idea is heady stuff. The Idea was a
religious one, since it was on the religious plane that
Dostoievsky believed Holy Russia could ultimately
resolve the conflicts of history, internal and external, but
that would hardly prevent its application to the
Revolutionary Russia that in fact followed. Anyway,
MacDiarmid's poem reflects the religious atmosphere of
post-war Europe, with its desperate hankering after
spiritual regeneration, sometimes in unlikely places. It is
thus appropriate enough that passages in the poem
remind one of Solovyov's concept of Godmanhood, and
assorted beliefs from what one might call alternative
religion as found in the Cabbala, as well as Dostoievsky's
version of Christianity, to which, according to Spengler,

a'—all   owretone — overtone
pit—put

the next thousand years would belong—hence MacDiarmid's reference to "this Christ o' the neist thoosand years." (139.)

Spengler's predestined historical cycles have a part to play in *A Drunk Man*, as does his antithesis of Appolonian and Faustian Man, which he developed from Nietzsche's concept of the Appolonian and the Dionysian, ultimately the opposing principles in whose perpetual strife the process of life consists. It was Nietzsche who declared that "one is fruitful only at the cost of being rich in contradictions," and there is a place of honour reserved for that very religious atheist in the poem, alongside Dostoievsky, who said he would be "with Christ against truth." The aspect of Nietzsche's thought most often adverted to in *A Drunk Man* is his ethic of self-realisation: "What does your conscience say?—You shall become what you are." This MacDiarmid extends from the individual to the nation. But the main link between Nietzsche and Dostoievsky in the poem is their insistence on cruelty, on suffering, psychologically associated with the sado-masochist theme, and philosophically asserted as the necessary condition of any higher human development. In this connection one may recall the early study of Dostoievsky, *The Cruel Genius*, by Mikhaylovsky, and the strain of thought in Nietzsche summed up in his statement that "almost everything that we call 'higher culture' is based upon the spiritualising and intensifying of cruelty."

> Ha'e I the cruelty I need,
> Contempt and syne contempt o' that,
> And still contempt in endless meed
> That I may never yet be caught
> In ony satisfaction, or
> Bird-lime that winna let me soar?   (145.)

neist – next	ony – any
ha'e – have	winna – won't
syne – then, next	

> Bite into me forever mair and lift
> Me clear o' chaos in a great relief
> Till, like this thistle in the munelicht growin',
> I brak in roses owre a hedge o' grief.   (113.)

Another thinker, Leo Shestov, should be mentioned here, not only because he believed that "Nietzsche has shown us the way: we must seek for that which is *above* pity, *above* the Good," but because MacDiarmid acknowledged him to be the 'master' who took him over "that frontier beyond which the might of general ideas ceases" to "try his luck with the idea of chaos."[14] The point in *A Drunk Man* at which the poet makes the leap into the Shestovian abyss beyond the rational, on the far side of good and evil, was intended, I think, as the high point of the whole poem: a section which shortly before publication he said he was rewriting in an attempt to project it on to "a different altitude of poetry altogether."[15] It certainly presents a line of thought which is amongst the most difficult to grasp, and it may be useful to make an attempt at that here.

This is where the poet turns to the most starkly arche-typal of his polar images, the Light and the Dark of the creation:

> 'Let there be Licht,' said God, and there was
> A little.   (148.)

Light is a flash in the pan, a spark that misfired in the cosmic dark, which is our natural element. Our short day between the two nights (before birth and after death) is not "illuminated" by the Light, and, most crucial of all, "Licht thraws nae licht upon itsel':" it reveals nothing about the nature of its existence or its origin in the Dark. (MacDiarmid's "text" here is taken from Susan Glaspell's *Berenice*: "Lights which only light themselves

mair – more
munelicht – moonlight

brak – break
thraws – throws

keep us from having light—from knowing what the darkness is.") Day is the false face of Night, and we are willing victims of what Nietzsche called "the will to deception." Even if there *is* a God who made the Light and also made such freaks as man, adapted to receive it, that deity is just the demi-urge of the creation, who changed nothing in the Dark by lighting up a tiny part of it, showing nothing that was not already there, and confusing even that.

Here one may recall Valéry's "Ébauche d'un Serpent," in which the Sun is declared to be a "glaring mistake," and a life-mask for death:

> Soleil, soleil! . . . Faute éclatante!
> Toi qui masques la mort, Soleil, . . .
> Tu gardes les coeurs de connaître
> Que l'univers n'est qu'un défaut
> Dans la pureté du Non-être!

"The universe is merely a blot on the purety of Non-being." That may be asserted from the Serpent's point of view, but MacDiarmid accepts its truth. And as for the life which the light of the sun produced on earth, culminating in mortal man, he says this is an aberration, a disease. It is not a matter of life being disrupted by death, but rather of death being infected with a localised and temporary rash of life.

Of the two poles of Chaos and Cosmos, then, it may well be the dark one of Chaos that is the positive and constructive—a thought that exercised the minds of Tyutchev and Shestov before it reached MacDiarmid. But again he provides a link with his hero, Dostoievsky, which helps to hold these shifting associations together in the poem:

> . . . only in the entire dark there's founts of
>   strength
> Eternity's poisoned draps can never file.   (147.)

draps – drops   file – pollute

This echoes the Drunk Man's plea in the previous section for a share of Dostoievsky's appalling genius, as one who, like the great Russian, must draw his sustenance from "The everloupin' fountain/That frae the Dark ascends." (138.)

MacDiarmid does not in the end succeed in revealing the nature of those mysterious, purposive qualities in Chaos which he says can be perceived by the rays of its black sun—"un affreux soleil noir d'où rayonne la nuit."[16] Nor, in the "Great Wheel" section of *A Drunk Man* which follows, does he succeed in joining issue with "the Will that raised the Wheel and spins it still"—in Nietzschean terms, the Will to Power by which the Wheel of Becoming is kept in motion; which MacDiarmid associates, like Yeats in *A Vision*, with the Great Year of the precession of the equinoxes. These are aims he could not possibly realise—which is why he makes the attempt. For him, the distinction of the human spirit is that, at whatever cost in suffering, it aims beyond its reach, for only thus can consciousness be extended. And "the function of art is the extension of human consciousness."[17]

Hence the supreme value of poetry for MacDiarmid, as for Nietzsche, hinted at near the end of *A Drunk Man* in an allusion to the new "organs" or modes of consciousness which the Universal Man (or Superman?) might develop:

> And organs may develop syne
> Responsive to the need divine
> O' single-minded humankin'.
>
> The function, as it seems to me,
> O' Poetry is to bring to be
> At lang, lang last that unity.   (163.)

Poetry is a mode by which the process of Becoming, or in other terms Evolution, can be furthered by man.

everloupin' – everleaping   frae – from

Whatever one may make of that mind-stretching sequence of ideas and allusions, "the existence of the world," as Nietzsche said, "can be justified only as an aesthetic phenomenon," and one is left, appropriately enough, with the poetry. It is the quality of the poetry which MacDiarmid is able to sustain in the longer, more abstruse stretches of *A Drunk Man*, in which his speculative stamina is tested to the limit, that crowns the achievement of the work, making it that rare thing, a genuine modern long poem. The more immediately attractive, shorter, separable items, though often drawn into the orbits of the dynamic symbols, *are*, after all, separable items. The strain on the master-symbol of the thistle, embodying so many contraries—"'A' the uncouth dilemmas o' oor natur'/Objectified in vegetable-maitter"—begins to tell at last. Some of his ways of seeing it run the gamut of "metaphysical" wit. It is the aborted foetus of Scotland, half soul and half skeleton; a company of Highland soldiers swallowed by green alligators with nothing but the pompoms of their Balmoral bonnets left to tell the tale; coloured ping-pong balls on water jets at a shooting gallery; a nervous system; a stricture in the groins of light; the visual equivalent of the sound of the bagpipes:

> Your leafs
> Mind me o' the pipes' lood drone
> —And a' your purple tops
> Are the pirly-wirly notes
> That gang staggerin' owre them as they groan.   (96.)

But there are times when one feels the poet falling back on sheer improvisation, and one strongly suspects it was a good thing that F. G. Scott was at hand to assist with the excision of material from the poem amounting to "at least a third more than its published bulk."[18]

oor – our
mind – remind

pirly-wirly notes – tiny grace-notes
gang – go

Certainly the idea of antisyzygy, whether in its Caledonian or universal form, is immensely fruitful. It informs the imagery in a way which accommodates the recent (in 1926) rediscovery of the wit of Donne (defined by Johnson as *discordia concors*, in which 'the most heterogeneous ideas are yoked by violence together'); the practice of the Russian "Imaginists," who specialised in juxtaposing the most vulgar images alongside the sublime; and the Expressionists' projection of the inner on the outer world. It provides a rationale for the Drunk Man's grinding changes of mood. And it energises the duality at the heart of human experience, issuing in endless antimonies of the real and the ideal, passion and intellect, body and soul, lust and love, beauty and ugliness, God and man, life and death, chaos and cosmos, being and essence, oblivion and eternity. But its process in the mind of the Drunk Man is romantically self-lacerating, its effect on the reader diminishing with familiarity. It is then that the longer, sustained passages are needed, and the poet duly begins the climb towards a visionary summit above the grotesque rockface where life and thought are trapped.

The human mind finds no ultimate answer to its questioning, of course. The Drunk Man leaves us in the dark. He drops the Great Wheel not with a bang but a whimper, and turns to his wife for comfort. MacDiarmid the intrepid cosmonaut leaves us with a row of asterisks on the page. Even the question of how to write a great national poem when you are unfortunate enough to be a Scotsman in 1926 is, in the words of Saintsbury deferring judgment on the Russian novelists, "taken to avizandum."

But that is not the end. If at the deepest level "an uttered thought is a lie,"[19] the world of thought remains in eternal silence unbroken by the Word. And MacDiarmid—rising above the paradox that this utterance about an uttered thought being a lie, if true, must itself be a lie—makes a splendid recovery, satisfying the reader simply by the quality of the poetry, which is there for all to read, and leaving us to reflect that the last antisyzygy is between tragedy and comedy—on which the Drunk Man's wife has the last word:

Yet ha'e I Silence left, the croon o'a'.

No'her, wha on the hills langsyne I saw
Liftin'a foreheid o'perpetual snaw.

No'her, wha in the how-dumb-deid o'nicht
Kyths, like Eternity in Time's despite.

No'her, withooten shape, wha's name is Daith,
No'Him, unkennable abies to faith
—God whom, gin e'er He saw a man, 'ud be
E'en mair dumfooner'd at the sicht than he.

—But Him, whom nocht in man or Deity,
Or Daith or Dreid or Laneliness can touch,
Wha's deed owre often and has seen owre much.

O I ha'e Silence left,
                    —'And weel ye micht,'
Sae Jean'll say, 'eftir sic a nicht!'

croon – crown	gin – if
wha – who	dumfooner'd – dumbfound-
langsyne – long ago	ered
snaw – snow	nocht – naught
how-dumb-deid -- silent dead	dreid – dread
(of night)	deed – died
kyths – shows, appears	owre – too
withooten – without	weel – well
unkennable – unknowable	micht – might
abies – except	sic – such

REFERENCES

1. D. \ Craig, \ *The \ Real Foundations*, p. 236.
2. Reported by C. M. Grieve, *Dunfermline Press*, 11 Feb. 1923.
3. B. Deutsch & A. Yarmolinsky, *Modern Russian Poetry*, London 1923, pp. 129–30.
4. D. S. Mirsky, *Modern Russian Literature*, London 1925, pp. 107–8.
5. *G.H.*, 12 March 1927, p. 4.
6. G. G. Smith, *Scottish Literature*, London 1919, pp. 20, 22, 23.
7. *F.M.*, 7 April 1934, p. 9.
8. Deutsch & Yarmolinsky, p. 70.
9. D. Daiches, "Introduction," *A Drunk Man* (1953), p. xiii.
10. B. Deutsch & A. Yarmolinsky, *Contemporary German Poetry*, London 1923, p. 110. The use MacDiarmid made of other such sources will repay study. These include J. Bithell, *Contemporary Belgian Poetry*, London 1911; *Contemporary French Poetry*, London 1912. Also D. S. Mirsky, *A History of Russian Literature*, London 1927, p. 168 (for "The Church of My Fathers"); *Pushkin*, New York 1926, p. 195 (for "Why I Became A Scottish Nationalist").
11. He deplored the use made in *A Vision* of the Great Year and other "paraphernalia of romanticism" (*N.A.*, 15 July 1926, p. 120), but used some of it himself in the Great Wheel section of *A Drunk Man* (published November 1926).
12. Mirsky, *Modern Russian Literature*, p. 48.
13. This, and much of the preceding passage, was worked up from a review of a book about Dostoievsky by his wife. See K. Buthlay, "Some Hints for Source-hunters," *S.L.J.*, Dec. 1978, pp. 50–66.
14. *L.P.*, pp. 40, 67.
15. Letter to George Ogilvie, 6 Aug. 1926.
16. Victor Hugo, "Bouche d'Ombre."
17. "Art and the Unknown," (1926), *S.E.*, p. 44.
18. Letter to George Ogilvie, 9 Dec. 1926.
19. Tyutchev, "Silentium."

CHAPTER IV

THE SNAKE AND THE WATER OF LIFE

I am conscious that, although my commentary on *A Drunk Man* may, I hope, help new readers to find their way through some of its more difficult passages, I have been able to put all too few of its immediate attractions on display. An inescapable problem in that respect is that the work's great distinction lies in the level of imaginative and technical excellence that the poet keeps bringing it up to, despite occasional lapses, throughout its formidable length, and this could only be conveyed through quotation on a massive scale not possible here.

It is quite otherwise with *To Circumjack Cencratus*, the much longer poem which followed in 1930. Nothing would be simpler than to pick out the best bits of *Cencrastus*, and very attractive some of them are, but this has to be resisted because it would give a false impression of the whole, which represents a very different order of achievement from that of its predecessor.

Yet MacDiarmid seems to have conceived it on the highest level. Only a couple of weeks or so after the publication of *A Drunk Man*, he was assuring his friend and former teacher, George Ogilvie, that *Cencrastus* would be "a much bigger thing . . . in every way." It would rise above the warring antinomies of the earlier poem and "move on a plane of pure beauty and pure music. It will be an attempt to move really mighty numbers, . . . ideally complementary to the *Drunk Man*—positive where it is negative, optimistic where it is pessimistic, and constructive where it is destructive."[1] At that time, he allowed that it would be "about a year at least" before the new work (already advertised as being "in preparation") would be ready for publication. In fact it took four years, and he then told the same correspondent:

> I did not do in it what I intended—I deliberately deserted my big plan, because I realised I had lots of elements in me, standing between me and really great work, I'd to get rid of—and I think I've done it. My next book will be a very different matter—with none of the little local and temporary references, personalities, political propaganda, literary allusiveness etc.[2]

Clearly he is suggesting that the sort of "elements" he lists had crept into *Cencrastus* simply because he had to get them out of his system, even at the cost of abandoning his plan. They include complaints about his job as a reporter in Montrose, domestic and financial worries, and disgust with the cultural state of Scotland, all of which might be associated with the unhappy state of affairs leading to his disastrous move from Scotland to London and Liverpool, the break-down of his marriage, unemployment, and other personal circumstances, of which Compton Mackenzie was to say that it was only by a miracle that any sort of book appeared at all. But the trouble is not just that such things got into the poem in the form of verse at an inferior or trivial level, dashed off in irritable frustration, or sometimes with forced, defensive humour. One also notes the inclusion of substantial items, such as "A Moment in Eternity" and the adapted translation of Rilke's *Requiem—Für eine Freundin* (reputedly based on a version by J. S. Buist), which disconcert the reader, not because of their inferiority, but because little or no attempt has been made to introduce them to their neighbours. When one adds to these such things as what appear to be scrapings of the barrel of his earlier English verse (offered amongst the specimens of "truly classical" poems of which he is most proud), and some dense patches of versified swatches of his reading, one must conclude that

one aspect of his "big plan" was unfortunately not abandoned: the determination at any rate to make *Cencrastus* a
bigger thing than *A Drunk Man* in sheer length. This
results in the reader coming to regard *Cencrastus* as a
"gallimaufry" in a perjorative sense not properly applic-
able to *A Drunk Man*, despite the fact that MacDiarmid
did make efforts to reorientate the poem when he decided
his first plan would not work.

His original intention was to circumjack Cencrastus in
the sense that "Cencrastus" (the name of a snake he found
in Jamieson) was the world-serpent or "the underlying
unifying principle of the cosmos" and "to circumjack"
(also in Jamieson) was derived from *circumjacere*, "to lie
round or about." Traces of the serpent as conceived on a
highly metaphysical level of "Godheid and Scottishness"
show through the published poem like a palimpsest. The
Unkent God is also there (or rather the mention of him is,
his whereabouts being naturally undisclosed), with
Solovyov on the spiritualisation of minerals, plants and
beasts, and the restoration in Man of the divine
androgyny; while Tyutchev's insistence on the need for
silence is again noised abroad:

> Silence is the only way,
> Speech squares aye less wi' fact.
> Silence—like Chaos ere the Word
> That gar'd the Play enact
> That sune to conscious thocht
> Maun seem a foolish dream.
> Nae Word has yet been said,
> Nae Licht's begun to gleam.   (218–9.)

But there is also a major new theme which is intended to
link up with Cencrastus on a different level: what
MacDiarmid called "the Gaelic Idea." This theme is not
stated strongly or clearly in the poem, a fact which may

gar'd – made   maun – must

reflect the poet's lack of confidence at this time in his ability to rise to a level of poetry commensurate with the challenge. But there is another factor involved: the difficulty of associating anything positive or humanly realizable with the original symbol of Cencrastus, which was by its very nature the most elusive of concepts, since, as he says repeatedly,

> There is nae movement in the warld like yours.

However, to the extent that the new theme can be linked with Cencrastus, it requires his movement to function historically, since the Gaelic Idea is to be the Celtic contribution to history as conceived by MacDiarmid. This is hinted at here and there, but so tentatively that when he does state his theme, more than a third of the way through the poem, the reader is very unlikely to perceive its bearing on the scattered mass of Celtic material and allusions in the work. Rather, he will be inclined to see it as a more or less isolated and eccentric political puzzle:

> If we turn to Europe and see
> Hoo the emergence o' the Russian Idea's
> Broken the balance o' the North and Sooth
> And needs a coonter that can only be
> The Gaelic Idea
> To mak' a parallelogram o' forces,
>   Complete the Defence o' the West,
> And end the English betrayal o' Europe.   (222–3.)

To grasp what he intends by this, one has to leave the poem and turn to MacDiarmid's prose. There one discovers that, at least as early as 1927, he could see the main hope of a Scottish revival not in Lowland Scotland but in the Gaelic heritage which Scotland shared with the other Celtic countries, most notably Ireland. It was to that heritage that "a return must be made before a foundation

hoo – how

can be secured for the creation of major forms either in arts or affairs."[3] His growing conviction of the radical significance of this idea was reinforced by various contacts, including his meetings with prominent literary and political figures in Ireland in 1928. And what emerges so obliquely in *Cencrastus* is a statement in vaguely political terms of his commitment to the revival of the Celtic ethos in Europe: not just a Scottish but a Celtic renascence.

The political scaffolding in the quoted passage came from Henri Massis's book, *The Defence of the West* (1927), in which the West is represented by Catholic Latin civilisation, threatened by the "dark barbarism" of "Bolshevism and Asiaticism," abetted by developments in post-war Germany. There are fuller statements of the idea in MacDiarmid's prose soon after *Cencrastus* was published. For example:

> The old balance of Europe—between North and South—has been disrupted by the emergence of Russia. How is a quadrilateral of forces to be established? England partakes too much of Teutonic and Mediterranean influences; it is a composite—not a 'thing-in-itself.' Only in Gaeldom can there be the necessary counter-idea to the Russian Idea—one that does not run wholly counter to it, but supplements, corrects, challenges and qualifies it. Soviet economics are confronted with the Gaelic system with its repudiation of usury which finds its modern expression in Douglas Economics. The dictatorship of the proletariat is confronted by the Gaelic Commonwealth with its aristocratic culture—the high place it gave to its poets and scholars. And so on.[4]

Now, in the poem, there are some indications of the aristocratic aspect of Gaelic culture, but the reader is hardly likely to suspect the significance of this for the Gaelic Idea so described. And without a footnote from the poet, one would not know that he had Douglas economics

in mind. But there would seem to be another difficulty.
"The Gaelic Idea" is balanced against "the Russian
Idea"—and how are we to reconcile Dostoievsky's
religiously-based conception of Russia's historic national
mission with what is now "the Soviet concept of things"?
MacDiarmid's answer is as follows:

> The point is that Dostoievski's was a great creative
> idea—a dynamic myth—and in no way devalued by the
> difference of the actual happenings in Russia from any
> Dostoievski dreamed or desired. So we in Scotland (in
> association with the other Gaelic elements with whose
> aid we may reduce England to a subordinate rôle in the
> economy of these islands) need not care how future
> events belie our anticipations so long as we polarize
> Russia effectively—proclaim that relationship between
> freedom and genius, between freedom and thought,
> which Russia is denying—help to rebalance Europe in
> accordance with our distinctive genius—rediscover and
> manifest anew our dynamic spirit as a nation.

This, however unmanifest to the reader, was intended
to be the new major theme of *Cencrastus*: the rediscovery of
the Celtic ethos and its expression in a dynamic myth, the
Gaelic Idea, to counter-balance the emergence of the
Russian Idea in its Soviet form. But the dynamism of the
myth could only be conveyed by using it effectively, which
is what MacDiarmid conspicuously fails to do in the
poem. Structure was never his strong point, on a large
scale, and it is especially weak here. The announcement of
the Gaelic Idea (222–3) needs to be firmly linked with the
related theme of "the unconscious goal of history," but the
latter occupies a section placed almost at the end of the
work (287–9), and there is little or nothing in the interven-
ing sixty-odd pages to encourage the reader to make the
necessary connection. This section uses material based on
Eduard von Hartmann's *Philosophy of the Unconscious*, with
special emphasis being put on the capacity of men of

genius to embody the aims of history, and even to achieve full consciousness of its "unconscious goal." But when it comes to the point of affirming the Gaelic Idea as this particular man of genius's contribution to the process, MacDiarmid is most uncharacteristically diffident:

> . . . Hoosoever petty I may be, the fact
> That I think Scotland isna dune yet proves
> There's something in it that fulfilment's lacked
> And my vague hope through a' creation moves. (288.)

We are given this "vague hope" instead of the "dynamic myth," the "great creative idea," because of the poet's lack of confidence in his ability to rise to the height of the creative act—not lack of confidence in the myth or idea as such, of which he said, "it does not matter a rap whether the whole conception of this Gaelic Idea is as far-fetched as Dostoievski's Russian Idea." All that finally mattered to him was that the Idea should issue in a great poem, since that itself could embody the myth in a form that might reawaken the Celtic world,

> Sae that my people frae their living graves
> May loup and play a pairt in History yet
> Wi' sufferin's mair like a Genius's than a slave's.

But that was not forthcoming. Nor could he get out of his present difficulties by trying to switch Cencrastus back on to the religious level via T. E. Hulme, or by borrowing ill-matched new imagery of sea and snake from an article in the *New Age*, brought in at the end of the poem.[5]

It is clear that one of the main reasons why his poem failed as a whole is that its solitary key-symbol of the serpent is not put to effective structural use, as was the thistle in *A Drunk Man*. One would have thought that the snake-motif so familiar in Celtic culture was crying out to be used for linking imagery between his metaphysical

dune – done   loup – leap
sae – so

speculations about Cencrastus and his explorations of the
Gaelic heritage, but about all he offers in that respect is a
rather sad reference to himself as a poet "Wha aince o'
verses like the serpent work/On Innis Draomich's crosses
dreamt." (196.) Similarly, he has numerous allusions to
Valéry in the poem (and steals some of his best lines from
him),[6] but, apart from a passing reference to the
smoothness of his snake that "maks cacophony of Valéry's
esses," he does not draw upon the abundant products of
the French poet's fascination with the archetypal serpent,
which would be most to his purpose here. Instead, he
takes the mysterious figure of Athikte, the dancer in
Valéry's *L'Âme et la Danse*, treats her in a manner which
can only make the reader confused and irritated, and
leaves her in the lurch, observing that

> . . . even the art o' MacDiarmid
> Leaves her a connached mermaid.   (233.)

In a long poem with no linear progression, coherence of
imagery can be especially valuable as a structural
element, as *A Drunk Man* plainly shows, and *Cencrastus*
suffers from the lack of this. For example, the problem of
the poet's language, and the need for a tradition to go with
it, to which he keeps recurring, is not linked with the
serpent tongue of Cencrastus, though he tells us near the
beginning of the poem that "the poet's hame is in the serpent's mooth."

Instead of the serpent, it is the mavis of Paval (Paible, in
North Uist) that announces this theme. The mavis comes
from a Gaelic song by John MacCodrum (translated by
John Stuart Blackie) and, metamorphosed into MacDiarmid in darker days, the bird stands "on the tap o' the hill"
where, he says,

> I'll sing as I sang in the past
> —If singin' depends upon will.

aince – once   connached – washed out

But will is not enough, as MacDiarmid is painfully recognising,

> For poetry's no' made in a lifetime
> And I lack a livin' past.

Also, one mavis doesn't make a renaissance, but

> There's nae sign o' a mate to be seen.

There is a strong contrast between the message MacDiarmid puts in the mouth of the bird and that of the original. The sadness of MacCodrum's mavis is only a memory of the past, and he goes on to celebrate the good that comes to him from his native land. But MacDiarmid's mavis knows that, although he has returned to the top of the hill, "the miracle canna last."

> I should ha'e stayed wi' the rest
> Doon in Coille Ghrumach still
> And no' ettled to be on the crest
> O' this bricht impossible hill.   (191–2.)

Coille Ghruamach, the "gloomy forest," is the setting for a poem called "*Am Bàrd an Canada*" by a Highland emigrant, John Maclean, who tells of his sufferings in Nova Scotia. The strength is leaving his heart and brain, he can no longer sing "the old songs of Albyn," the Gaelic is dying. And these are the associations which darken MacDiarmid's poem.

However, as we are told later, *on áird tuaidh in chabhair* ("help comes from the northern airt"), for it is there that the Scottish poet can yet recover his lost Gaelic background, "get down to *Ur-motives*," and "get back behind the [European] Renaissance" to his own classical sources. But this involves the inescapable problem of language:

doon – down   bricht – bright
ettled – aimed

> O wad at least my yokel words
> Some Gaelic strain had kept! . . .
> Curse on my dooble life and dooble tongue
> —Guid Scots wi' English a' hamstrung—
> Speakin' o' Scotland in English words
> As it were Beethoven chirpt by birds.   (225, 236.)

There is, for the vast majority of Scotsmen, a linguistic
block between them and their Gaelic *Ur-motives*, and we
are not convinced by MacDiarmid's "haulf-English" in
this poem that there is still

> Time eneuch . . . to seek the Omnific Word
>   In Jamieson yet,
> Or the new Dictionary in the makin' noo,
>   Or coin it oorsels!   (223.)

The "new Dictionary" is the *Scottish National Dictionary*,
begun at that time, a little late in the day. MacDiarmid's
description of his language in *Cencrastus* as "hauf-English"
is accurate enough. It is a thin mixture, which, while close
to actual modern Scots speech, is deployed without much
vitality, in contrast to the rich variety of Scots handled
with such verve and flexibility in *A Drunk Man*. But
MacDiarmid's biggest limitation is not perhaps the
language he is using but the language he cannot use:
Gaelic, the right language for a man who wants to stake
the claims of the Gaelic Idea.

His knowledge of Gaelic seems to have been based on a
bare smattering picked up from a relative in childhood,[7]
and the source of his references to and quotations from
Irish poets in *Cencrastus* was Aodh de Blácam's *Gaelic
Literature Surveyed* (1929). However, there is more to some
of the Irish references than at first may be apparent. For
example, one of the hottest controversies in Scotland at
that time was the "Irish Invasion" of the country which

guid – good   oorsels – ourselves
eneuch – enough

raised acute religious, political, and economic issues there, and it is only in that context that one can fully understand MacDiarmid's oblique reference to *Tabhroidh chugam cruit mo ríogh* ("Bring me the harp of my king"). This is a poem by Gilbride Albanach MacNamee concerning a treasured Irish harp which somehow found its way to Scotland, where its adopted guardian refused to part with it. "Dear to me (my due by birth), the fair forest of Alba," he said. "Strange it is, yet more I love this tree from Eire's woodlands." And it is his "honey mouth" that is blessed by his countryman, MacDiarmid, who intends by his reference to "the branch of Ireland growing among us" to indicate that his Celtic interests are not something remote from present reality but relevant to the urgent questions of the day. From his point of view, "the growth of Catholicism [in Scotland] and the influx of the Irish are alike welcome, as undoing those accompaniments of the Reformation which have lain like a blight on Scottish arts and affairs."[8]

Nevertheless, there is ample evidence in the poem of the strain on his resources imposed by the attempt to make live contact with the Gaelic past, whether of Ireland or of Scotland, and for long stretches one has the impression that his heart is not really in the struggle. There is a tiredness about the poem, betrayed by the language, and MacDiarmid has to concede that he cannot absorb the ethos of Gaeldom in the way that Grieve did that of Lowland Scotland:

> Fain through Burns' clay MacMhaighstir's fire
> To glint within me ettled.
> It stirred, alas, but couldna kyth,
> Prood, elegant and mettled.   (225.)

His tribute to MacMhaighstir (the great Scots Gaelic poet, Alexander MacDonald) is not carried through in

ettled – struggled   prood – proud
kyth – show, appear   mettled – spirited

Cencrastus, like so much else. A more adequate tribute was to be the translation of MacDonald's "Birlinn of Clanranald" which he made later, with the help of Sorley Maclean, the most distinguished contemporary Gaelic poet, who in turn owed much to MacDiarmid.

The technical virtuosity of the Gaelic poetic tradition was what most impressed MacDiarmid, but he was not able to make much of that sort of technique work for him. Taking his bearings from Daniel Corkery's *Hidden Ireland* (1925), he saw in the Celtic tradition a way of "getting back behind the Renaissance" to a deeper conception of classicism than that advocated by Hulme or Eliot (both of whom he echoes in the course of the poem). Like so many modern romantics, he yearned after the classical. But the practical results of this in *Cencrastus* do not go much beyond a tentative Scots Anthology to set against the Greek. Some of this is excellent of its kind, but it is a very long way from the "creation of major forms" which he expected to result from a return to the Gaelic roots of Scotland.

The form in which he projected his next major work has a distinctly romantic look about it, with a suggestion of Wordsworth's *Prelude*. It was planned to be a huge autobiographical poem in five volumes called *Clann Albann*,[9] and he intended to include in the first volume of that never-completed work the contents of *First Hymn to Lenin and Other Poems* (1931), *Scots Unbound and Other Poems* (1932), the *Second Hymn to Lenin*, which was published separately in pamphlet form in 1932, and numerous other items which remained in periodicals until they were resurrected in recent years—some of these last being of the highest quality. This indicates that, aside from any other reason why he never carried out his plans for *Clann Albann*, MacDiarmid did not get some even of his best work into the small volumes he managed to publish after *Cencrastus*. His first four volumes of poetry had been published by the venerable Scottish firm of Blackwood (who one suspects were not sufficiently in command of the Scots language to take in some of the things their author was saying in *A Drunk Man*—but all honour to them anyway). Now he was depending on the firm he worked for briefly in London, and a small publisher in Stirling.

It is significant that the two Hymns to Lenin (a third appeared many years later) were intended to be placed in "The Muckle Toon," the first volume of *Clann Albann*. The tendency has been to treat the Hymns as evidence of a sudden switch by MacDiarmid to writing political verse in the narrow sense (in accordance with the stereotyped account of English poetry in the Thirties), and for long enough, if he was known at all in England, it was as such a writer, intent on Communist propaganda. But, although the "First Hymn" hails Lenin's revolution as the greatest turning-point in history since Christ, even if like Christ he was "pairtly wrang," the "Second Hymn" tells one a great deal more about MacDiarmid's conception of poetry than it does about politics or Lenin, whose taste in verse was deplorably conservative, and who is given a lecture on the art he so undervalued:

> Your knowledge in your ain sphere
> Was exact and complete
> But your sphere's elementary and sune by
> As a poet maun see't. . . .

> Unremittin', relentless,
> Organized to the last degree,
> Ah, Lenin, politics is bairns' play
> To what this maun be!   (326, 328.)

The poem is certainly not a hymn to Lenin in any usual meaning of the word. And, although MacDiarmid was ere long to commit himself to Communism, his vision of that was inclined to be as peculiar to himself as was his vision of other great Ideas that possessed him.

Together with the other poems he planned to include in

"The Muckle Toon," he associated the two "Hymns" with his birthplace, Langholm; and in so far as they have a specifically political orientation, he said "they are in logical sequence from the radicalism of that Border burgh," and are "presented merely as starting points for the attitudes developed from book to book."[10] But he did not see them as being primarily political poems; otherwise he would have designated them for inclusion in the *second* volume of *Clann Albann* as he planned it.

No doubt there could have been ulterior motives for MacDiarmid letting it be known to his critics that "none of the opinions expressed are necessarily his own at all; all these poems are part of a big scheme in which the diverse points of view expressed will be balanced against each other."[11] But that statement accords well enough with the basic attitude be held at the time, in opposition to

all fixed opinions—all ideas that are not entertained just provisionally and experimentally—every attempt to regard any view as permanent . . . every denial of the relativity and transience of all thought, any failure to "play with ideas"—and above all the stupid (since self-stultifying) idea that ideas are not of prime consequence in their qualitative ratio and that it is possible to be over-intellectual . . . .[12]

In any case, it is a fact that the attitude he adopted towards Lenin and revolutionary Communism is best understood if one sees the first two "Hymns" in the context of the other poems which he was writing then. These show that he was especially preoccupied with the source of "inspiration" and the mysterious factors that go to produce "genius," because he believed the hope of mankind to lie in the possibility of evolving a race of men to whom what is now called "genius" would be the norm. The tremendous significance of Lenin's revolution (*and* Douglas's economics, in the existing situation) was that it promised to clear "bread-and-butter problems" out of the way and establish much more favourable conditions for this all-important evolutionary process. "If Communism did not mean *that*, . . . if it only meant raising the economic level of everybody until it was as high as that of the wealthiest man in the world to-day, I would not move a little finger to assist in the process."[13]

> Wanted a technique for genius! Or, at least,
> A means whereby a' genius yet has done
> 'll be the startin' point o' a' men's lives,
> No' zero, as if life had scarce begun,
> But to owrecome this death sae faur ben in
>   Maist folk needs the full floo'er o' Lenin.
>
> Be this the measure o' oor will to bring
> Like cruelty to a' men—nocht else 'll dae;
> The source o' inspiration drooned in bluid
> If need be, owre and owre, until its ray
> Strengthens in a' forever or's hailly gane
>   As noo save in an antrin brain.
>   ("The Burning Passion," 305.)

The "cruelty" that has to be brought to all men is the suffering of genius, the necessary concomitant of any step upwards on the evolutionary ladder since Man has become aware (however dimly and partially) of the ladder itself. And on the political level the cruelty is that of "the Cheka's horrors," amorally justified on the theory that the end justifies the means, since revolution is seen as a way of speeding up the evolution of mankind.

> Oh, it's nonsense, nonsense, nonsense,
> Nonsense at this time o' day
> That breid-and-butter problems
> S'ud be in ony man's way.

faur – far	bluid – blood
ben in – within	hailly – wholly
floo'er – flower	antrin – occasional
drooned – drowned	s'ud – should

They s'ud be like the tails we tint
On leavin' the monkey stage;
A' maist folk fash aboot's alike
Primaeval to oor age.   ("Second Hymn," 325.)

However deplorable the strong streak of inhumanity in
MacDiarmid's writing—and the other side of that is the
great kindness he showed to innumerable people in the
flesh—one cannot just attack it on the political level. His
all-consuming passion is for the source of "genius," and
the enlargement of consciousness to grasp it, so that his
poetry is forever straining to get on to an "inhuman" level.
The source has nothing human about it: it is in God, as
understood by his "master" Shestov—a Being that has
nothing to do with standards of morality or logic, yet is
ultimately the only thing worth seeking.

In returning imaginatively to "The Muckle Toon" of
Langholm, MacDiarmid was probing the source of his
own genius, about which (in print) he showed little doubt.
The imagery of these poems is drawn largely from
boyhood memories of places and people, particularly his
relatives, and light is sometimes shed on the poems by the
little-known Scots prose pieces he had contributed to
periodicals some years before.[14] The prose and poetry
mutually confirm how strong the autobiographical
element was in his work at the time.

The dominant symbolism in the poems is of water, since
"a perfect maze of waters is aboot the Muckle Toon," and
in following the streams of his boyhood to their source, he
passes from the mystery of genius to the origin and evolution of life itself:

And aye the force that's brocht life up
Frae chaos to the present stage
Creates new states as ill for us
As oors for eels to gauge.   ("Water of Life," 317.)

tint – lost   brocht – brought
fash – bother, fuss

One begins to realise how that characteristic sense of the newly created world which is imprinted on so many of his poems comes from the actual experience of his childhood. The streams of the Wauchope, Esk, and Ewes are set flowing again in "Water of Life" (*First Hymn*) and are given their rhythmical apotheosis in the "Water Music" of *Scots Unbound*:

> Lively, louch, atweesh, atween,
> Auchimuty or aspate,
> Threidin' through the averins
> Or bightsom in the aftergait. (333.)

"The promise that there'll be nae second Flood" he takes "wi' a' the salt I've saved since then," linking the fierce religion of his ancestors with those wonderful Waterside folk who are celebrated in the finest of the Scots prose sketches, "The Waterside:"

The Waterside folk kept skitin' this way and that. There was neither peace nor profit in their lives. They couldna settle. Their kind of life was like the dipper's sang. It needit the skelp and slither o' runnin' water like the bagpipes' drone to fill oot the blanks. Withoot that it was naething but a spraichle o' jerky and meaningless soonds . . . . That's what I mean when I say that the Waterside folk were brainless craiturs. Brains were nae use there. To dae onything ava they'd to use something faur quicker than thocht—something as auld as water itsel'. And thocht's a dryland thing and a gey recent yin at that.[15]

louch – downcast
atweesh – betwixt
atween – between
auchimuty – mean, thin
aspate – in flood
threidin' – threading
averins – cloudberries
bightsom – ample

aftergait – outcome
skitin' – flying off at a tangent
skelp – slap
spraichle – scramble
craturs – creatures
ava – at all
gey – very, rather
yin – one

Clearly, these are the same characters of whom he says in "Water of Life:"

> They were like figures seen on fountains whiles.
> The river made sae free wi' them—poored in and oot
> O' their een and ears (no' mooths) in a' its styles,
> Till it clean scooped the insides o' their skulls
>   O' a' but a wheen thochts like gulls.
>
> Their queer stane faces and hoo green they got!
> Juist like Rebecca in her shawl o' sly.
> I'd never faur to gang to see doon there
> A wreathèd Triton blaw his horn or try,
> While at his feet a clump o' mimulus shone
>   Like a dog's een wi' a' the world a bone.   (318–9.)

Norman MacCaig has shrewdly remarked that the words 'or try' in the above quotation could only have been written by MacDiarmid. They bear his signature. So does the last line of the following:

> Spring to the North has aye come slow
> But noo dour winter's like to stay
>   For guid,
>   And no' for guid![16]

What these examples have in common is the "literal" feeling for words that was so strong in this poet. It is a special aspect of an insatiable interest in words as such which led him to devour dictionaries and construct verbal *tours de force* like "Scots Unbound," "Tarras," "Water Music," "Balefire Loch," and parts of "Depth and the Chthonian Image." The first of these is subtitled "*Divertissement philologique*," and that is essentially what it is, although it may be noted how the river Esk slips into the picture (as into so many of the poems of this period)

een – eyes   sly – green slime on water
mooths – mouths   gang – go
wheen – few   blaw – blow

and turns his thoughts back to his Muse once again. The reader has to do his homework with Jamieson and others at his elbow before he is in a position to appreciate this "exercise of delight in the Scots sense of colour" and, to a lesser extent, smell and taste. It is an "exercise" for the reader too: a kind of verbal gymnastics not everyone will care to take up.

"Water Music" is in a different category, not because its vocabulary is any easier in itself, but because it is rhythmically so powerful and musically such a delight that the literal meaning is only an added satisfaction, rather than a necessary condition of enjoyment. Here MacDiarmid has culled the lexicon for pairs of Scots words with contrary or at any rate widely different meanings, and developed a verbal dialectic with a rhythm powerful enough to carry them along with great verve while at the same time bouncing them off one another, very often with alliteration making the initial point of contact. One reads first of all by ear, checks the meaning of words one has not been able to guess or "feel," and then returns to take still greater pleasure from the music. The poem is in two parts, the second not managing to sustain the sheer brilliance of the first but full of good things nevertheless, and it begins and ends with this injunction to James Joyce:

> Wheesht, wheesht, Joyce, and let me hear
> Nae Anna Livvy's lilt,
> But Wauchope, Esk and Ewes again,
> Each wi' its ain rhythms till't.

It is a brave man who invokes comparison with the author of "Anna Livia Plurabelle" in the handling of rhythm. MacDiarmid carries it off splendidly:

wheesht – hush   till't – to it
ain – own

And you've me in your creel again,
   Brim or shallow, bauch or bricht,
Singin' in the mornin',
   Corrieneuchin' a' the nicht.   (335.)

What has been called his "infallible ear for Scots vocables" is still operating at peak efficiency in "Milk-Wort and Bog-Cotton" (1932), the last and, to my mind, loveliest of his great Scots lyrics:

Cwa' een like milk-wort and bog-cotton hair!
I love you, earth, in this mood best o' a'
When the shy spirit like a laich wind moves
And frae the lift nae shadow can fa'
Since there's nocht left to thraw a shadow there
Owre een like milk-wort and milk-white cotton hair.

Wad that nae leaf upon anither wheeled
A shadow either and nae root need dern
In sacrifice to let sic beauty be!
But deep suroondin' darkness I discern
Is aye the price o' licht. Wad licht revealed
Naething but you, and nicht nocht else concealed.
                                  (331.)

The first two words of the poem show that he did not need to go "dictionary-dredging" to find effects in colloquial Scots unobtainable in English: try substituting "Come away eyes . . ." Anyone picking up the echo of Wordsworth's "Waggoner" in the "shy spirit" of the third line will recognise the aptness of the allusion at a deep level. The variation on the opening line that occurs in the last line of the first stanza is an example of consummate verbal musicianship. The unrhymed third line gives his

in your creel – under your
  spell
bauch – dull
corrieneuchin' – gossiping
cwa' – come away

laich – low
lift – sky
nocht – naught
thraw – throw
dern – hide

individual stamp to a conventional-looking stanza form.
And the closing lines show (or rather *sound*) what he meant
when he said:

> the sang in my hert
> Coonts ilka shadow frae nicht to nocht.   (232.)

Those qualities of language which appeal to the ear are
naturally of special importance in the poems that employ
a very unfamiliar vocabulary of dictionary Scots. The ear
has to bridge *lacunae* in the sense, and, in particular, the
rhythm must keep the strange words from clogging and
clotting when they are used very thickly; otherwise the
reader may be oppressed with a sense of mere verbalism.
"Tarras" is a great *tour de force* in this respect—a celebra-
tion of "the auld vulture" of the bog, the earth-mother and
bed-mate of "the hairy ones," that again will stand comparison with the Joyce of *Finnegans Wake*, though of course
there is a fundamental difference in the linguistic techniques by which the two authors get their effects.

MacDiarmid was also to use Scots for a new purpose in
his "Ex-Parte Statement on the Project of Cancer," which
makes science a springboard for imaginative speculation.
And, in addition to all this, he produced a remarkable
example of a notoriously difficult form of art: a proletarian
poem by a literary intellectual. In "The Seamless
Garment," talking to a Langholm mill-worker, the poet
explains his view of Lenin and Rilke in terms of weaver
and machine, and of the proverbial wisdom of the
housewife, ending shrewdly by adopting the weaver's test
of good cloth for his own poetry. There is no condescen-
sion in this. It is straight man-to-man stuff, in which the
limitation of modern colloquial Scots—the fact that it
tends to be associated largely with working folk who have
had least in the way of formal education—is seen to have
its own virtue:

ilka – every

Are you equal to life as to the loom?
  Turnin' oot shoddy or what?
Claith better than man? D'ye live to the full,
  Your poo'ers a' deliverly taught?
Or scamp a'thing else? Border claith's famous.
Shall things o' mair consequence shame us?   (312.)

MacDiarmid's subsequent volumes contain relatively few poems in Scots. Though he never completely stopped writing in that language (and indeed in the 'Fifties, and even later, told the present writer that he was searching for a theme to hold together a long poem in Scots on the lines of *A Drunk Man*), there was clearly at this point a change in direction which led him to write mainly in English again.

claith – cloth   deliverly – continuously

REFERENCES

1. Letter to George Ogilvie, 6/8/26.
2. Letter to G. Ogilvie, 16/12/30.
3. *The Present Condition of Scottish Arts and Affairs* (a pamphlet reprinting an article which appeared in 1927), p. 7.
4. "The Caledonian Antisyzygy and the Gaelic Idea" (1931–2). In *S.E.*, p. 67.
5. 289–92. Cf. Hulme, *Speculations*, London 1960, p. 34; Filioque, "The Great Sea-Serpent," *N.A.*, 11 March 1926, pp. 223–4. (The latter noted by R. B. Watson.)
6. 281–2. Cf. P. Valéry, *Une Soirée avec Monsieur Teste* and *Lettre d'Émilie Teste*. (MacDiarmid used translated material from Valéry and others found in W. Drake, *Contemporary European Writers*, London [1929].)
7. See *L.P.*, p. 5.
8. *Albyn* (1927), p. 11.
9. See *M.S.*, July 1931, p. 107; *S.O.*, 12 Aug. 1933, p. 10.
10. *S.O.*, 12 Aug. 1933, p. 10.
11. *S.O.*, 27 Jan. 1933, p. 11.
12. "The Caledonian Antisyzygy . . . ," *S.E.*, p. 68.
13. *L.P.*, p. 237.
14. See *G.H.*, 12 Mar., 16 Apr., 16 Jul., 27 Aug. 1927. *S.O.*, 19 Mar., 14 May, 10 Oct. 1927; 22 Sep. 1928. *S.M.*, Apr. 1927. (Four of these in *The Uncanny Scot*, ed. K. Buthlay, London 1968.)
15. *The Uncanny Scot*, pp. 43–4.
16. *Cencrastus*, 204.

CHAPTER V

STONES AND SKULLS

When the *Stony Limits* collection appeared in 1934, it confirmed a tendency already evident in MacDiarmid's recent contributions to periodicals whereby he had been writing his poems alternately in a rather thin variety of Scots or in English, with a growing preference for the latter. In the following year, only the title-poem of a collection of nearly fifty in *Second Hymn to Lenin and Other Poems* was in Scots, and it had been written at least three years before. Thereafter he wrote in English, with very few exceptions.

The picture is clear, a little too clear. For in MacDiarmid's periodical the *Voice of Scotland* for September and December 1947, eight poems from the *Second Hymn* volume appeared in Scots versions as parts of a long "Ode to All Rebels." And internal evidence showed that the Scots versions must have preceded the English ones, which suggested in turn that the whole of the "Ode" might have been written prior to 1935. That this was in fact the case was confirmed by the poet only in 1956, when he revealed that his publishers had deleted the complete poem from the manuscript of *Stony Limits*.

The 'Ode to All Rebels' represented the longest sustained performance MacDiarmid had achieved since *A Drunk Man*, which it resembles in some respects, especially in the opening sections, where sex is the dominant theme. This, along with some passages that might be regarded as blasphemous by a nervous lawyer, is presumably the reason why his publishers rejected it. The simple colloquial Scots in which most of it is written would

be much easier for the censorial mind to grasp than the
language of *A Drunk Man*. The same is true of "Harry
Semen," deleted from the same manuscript, though it did
appear in a magazine in 1933. It presents in vivid physical
detail the poet's fascinated revulsion at the wasteful and
random process of insemination by which he was conceived—and, typically, proceeds to a little speculation
about Christ's conception. "Harry Semen" is indeed one
of his most powerful poems; and the "Ode" shows that he
was still at that time capable of recovering a fair part of the
ground lost by *Cencrastus* in his "gallimaufry" form of
thought-narrative interspersed with lyrics. Taken
together with such substantial and accomplished pieces as
"By Wauchopeside" and "Whuchulls," left uncollected
in periodicals, these represent a very considerable
achievement in Scots; and the view sometimes put
forward, that he abandoned Scots for English at that time
because he had found it linguistically inadequate, is
obviously simplistic.

At the same time, the drift towards English—a cause of
angry frustration in *Cencrastus*—was no longer, on
occasion, being resisted. The final section of the "Ode,"
for example, draws to an impressive conclusion in that
language:

> Your song, O God, that none dare hear
> Save the insane and such as I
> Apostates from humanity
> Sings out in me with no more fear
> Than one who thinks he has the world's ear
>   From his padded cell
> —Insane enough, with you so near,
>   To want, like you, the world as well!   (512.)

The question of which language to use does not appear
to imply any momentous decision to abandon one in
favour of the other, and the impression one gets is of

MacDiarmid graduating towards English in response to some inner instinct which finally tells him he can no longer "follow up the *Drunk Man* line." Much later, he was to say that this situation was brought about by the series of crises in his personal life at the time.[1]

Apparently there was a partial blockage of the emotional springs that had sustained the lyric intensity and rhythmical flow of *A Drunk Man*. At any rate, the turning to English accompanied an approach to poetry in which the lyrical element was no longer relied upon to anything like the same extent.

The *Clann Albann* project was put aside, and so also was the plan for a 'companion volume' to *A Drunk Man* called *The Frontier: Or the War with England*, which seems in any case to have been a very shaky affair.[2] MacDiarmid became particularly interested in the possibilities of science for poetry—largely non-lyrical possibilities, of course—and after a few experiments in mixing scientific terminology with his synthetic Scots, he concentrated on using that terminology within the context of standard English. This was a logical move, since the intensive use of a specialised scientific diction in English verse was quite novel, and involved a sufficient number of problems in itself, without the added complication of importing all the scientific or technical terms into Scots. Considered as a distinct, fully national language, Scots had practically ceased to develop its vocabulary before modern science got under way, and it had very little of its own to offer later to the terminology of the industrial revolution.

The procedure of simply giving English scientific terms a Scottish accent was not of much account to MacDiarmid, though there could be certain advantages to it, one might think, if one wanted like Wordsworth to domesticate science. On the other hand, if, as MacDiarmid had said a dozen years before, "the problem is to determine what 'motor-car' would have been in the Doric had the Doric . . . become an all-sufficient independent language,"[3] he no longer thought that such problems, multiplied over and over again, could be solved by him or even by his generation. As he put it later:

> We have an enormous leeway to make up. I think the resources of Scots are adequate to the purpose; I think we can apply them. But it is not a job that can be done by one man or perhaps even in one lifetime. It may take several generations of intensive work along that line.[4]

In the meanwhile, he applied himself to the existing scientific terminology of English as offering a possibility of fresh linguistic sustenance that the English poets themselves had hardly begun to be aware of. Strictly scientific terms have obvious limitations which in practice restrict the effects he was able to get from them. The typical scientific vocabulary is very similar in languages which are in other aspects highly diversified, having been built up by very similar, deliberately chosen methods from ready-made units of (usually) Latin and Greek. The vast majority of such terms are products of a process which, of all kinds of word-formation, is the least concerned with the inner life of the native sound-system. From a poetic point of view, to use Pound's distinctions, there is a very limited range of *melopoeia*, of variety and suggestiveness of sound-qualities. The tendency in science towards abstraction militates against *phanopoeia*, "a casting of images upon the visual imagination." And then there is *logopoeia*: " 'the dance of the intellect among words,' that is to say, it employs words not only for their direct meaning, but it takes account in a special way of habits of usage, of the context we *expect* to find with the word, its usual concomitants, of its known acceptances, and of ironical play."[5] Where *logopoeia* is concerned, MacDiarmid's scientific terminology has an initial shock-effect, but eventually tends to monotony, because the extended use of such terms in poetry nearly always involves a context in which we would not normally expect to find these words, and where their usual concomitants are nearly always absent. Also, it is a basic principle of the formation of scientific terms that they should clearly denote one single meaning: they are made on purpose to discourage word-play.

When MacDiarmid extended his lexical range by going beyond the strictly scientific and technical to make use of what he called "recondite elements of the English vocabulary" wherever these existed, a restriction as to *logopoeia* continued to apply. Familiarity with the words' usage is a necessary condition for the development of "ironical play" on a level at which most readers will be ready to respond, and MacDiarmid's recondite elements are by definition unfamiliar. However, the other restrictions need not apply to anything like the same extent.

What he attempted, in some of the poems in *Stony Limits* and elsewhere, was to draw on these lexical resources for a new kind of poetic diction. If his Scots had been "synthetic," this was his "synthetic English." And he could use it on occasion very attractively. Here is a mild example, the closing lines of "In the Caledonian Forest," where his subject keeps him fairly close to the more conventional area of poetic imagery in the natural world, and leads him to include a couple of Scots words in the amalgam:

> The gold edging of a bough at sunset, its pantile
>   way
> Forming a double curve, tegula and imbrex in one,
> Seems at times a movement on which I might be
>   borne
> Happily to infinity; but again I am glad
> When it suddenly ceases and I find myself
> Pursuing no longer a rhythm of duramen
> But bouncing on the diploe in a clearing between
>   earth and air

Or headlong in dewy dallops or a moon-spairged
    fernshaw
Or caught in a dark dumosity or even
In open country again watching an aching
    spargosis of stars.   (392.)

Having relished the sound of "an aching spargosis of
stars," readers may have the metaphor implicit in the
Milky Way brought home to them, on learning that
"spargosis" means "a great distention of the breasts with
milk." And there are more of such happy discoveries to be
made here and in other poems. At his best, MacDiarmid is
illustrating an idea of which he was aware in a European
context—an idea expressed at this time by Karl Vossler:

> The technical languages as well as the national
> languages are dependent on the poetry inherent in their
> subject and their interests. Why should not . . . science
> as well as hunting, the exactitudes of definitions as well
> as the mist of dreams have a specific poetry? One only
> needs to feel them and listen to their sound.[6]

But MacDiarmid's real successes in this line tend to be
scattered here and there amongst the poems. In some of
his more drastic experiments, the esoteric diction
insulates the poem from the familiar world of the senses
and the emotions—including most aesthetic emotions
—the words being placed like so many cryptic pieces on
the chess-board of the poet's mind. A very good dictionary
will supply names for the pieces, but not much more than
that.[7] Only as they are moved in and out of the shifting
gambits of thought can they begin to exist in rhythmic
relationships—a rhythm that appeals more to the brain
than to the ear. It is as though the poet has to put connota-
tions into the words, instead of the usual procedure of
drawing them out. And once the initial novelty has worn
off, the game becomes excessively tiring.

MacDiarmid did not play it very often, however. His method with experimental techniques was to push them immediately to the extreme, as if to see how much they could stand. And in this case the breaking-point was quickly reached. When everything is more or less equally unfamiliar, there is nothing left for the unfamiliarity to refer back to. And especially where the terminology of the sciences is concerned, one remembers that the poet had just thrown an anarchist 'Ode' in the teeth of

> A' the men o' science, the enemies o' truth . . .
> A' that expect clear explanations,
> Fixed standards and reasonable methods. (507–8.)

As a matter of fact, one of the poems in *Stony Limits* uses the terminology of science to attack scientific rationalism. MacDiarmid had said, back in 1923, that he was "quite certain that the imagination had some way of dealing with the truth which the reason had not, and that commandments delivered when the body is still and the reason silent are the most binding that the souls of men can ever know."[8] Now, in the poem "Thalamus," he translated this perception into terms of the anatomy of the brain, saying that it was from the "older, darker, less studied regions of cranial anatomy" that there came

> The truths that all great thinkers have seen
> At the height of their genius—and then
> Spent most of their days denying
> Or trying to scale down to mere reason's ken
>   —The height to which all life must tend
>   And securely hold at the end.
>
> But proud of their cortex few
> Have glimpsed the medial nuclei yet
> Of their thalamus—that Everest in themselves
> Reason should have explored before it
>   As the corpora geniculata before any star
>   To know what and why men are.   (413.)

His own special scientific interest at this time, living in
Shetland, became geology. One of his very few compa-
nions there was a geologist, with whom he went exploring
the little islands around Whalsay. And his sense of
solitude and exiled remoteness in that treeless landscape
brought him close in spirit to Charles Doughty, the
solitary traveller and neglected poet, who had also
interested himself deeply in that science. Hence what
MacDiarmid ironically calls the "little array of Geology's
fal-de-las" which he brings to Doughty's grave in his
noble elegy, "Stony Limits." Apart from Hopkins, on a
much smaller scale, Doughty was the one great, pioneering, indeed prophetic poet he felt England had to offer him
as a spiritual companion in other, more arduous explorations; and the imagery of the poem takes in even the
geology of the mountains of the moon (which "allures
such spirits as ours"), before he launches into his final
resounding tribute:

> Not since Ezekial has that faw sun ringed
> A worthier head; red as Adam you stood
> In the desert, the horizon with vultures
>   black-winged,
> And sang and died in this still greater
>   solitude
> Where I sit by your skull whose emptiness is
>   worth
> The sum of almost all the full heads now on
>   Earth
> —By your roomy skull where most men might
>   well spend
> Longer than you did in Arabia, friend!   (422.)

The geological terms in "Stony Limits" do not seem to
me to succeed in carrying out what was wanted of them,
since rather too often they remain on the surface of the
poem, like decoration. In "On A Raised Beach," on the

other hand, there is at the entrance to the poem a great
pile of stony words which many readers must have found
excessively massive:

> All is lithogenesis—or lochia,
> Carpolite fruit of the forbidden tree,
> Stones blacker than any in the Caaba,
> Cream-coloured caen-stone, chatoyant pieces,
> Celadon and corbeau, bistre and beige,
> Glaucous, hoar, enfouldered, cyathiform,
> Making mere faculae of the sun and moon . . . .
>
> (422.)

The trouble is, there are another seventeen lines of this
still to go, and the dictionary gets heavier the oftener one
has to lift it. However, a growing number of readers have
not let that stop them from finding their way into the
poem, and its reputation has likewise grown. Monolithic
in a good sense, it is itself a massive piece of work, now
widely regarded as MacDiarmid's major achievement in
English.

One might indicate the taking-off point for the poem by
a remark of Keyserling's: "Once again I probe into the
dead stone as a geologist, in order to solve the significance
of the living."[9] Science has taught MacDiarmid at least
one great lesson:

> What happens to us
> Is irrelevant to the world's geology
> But what happens to the world's geology
> Is not irrelevant to us.   (428.)

However, it is only to be expected of this poet that science
will take him into other, more metaphysical regions.

When the reader has picked his way through the first
section, the stones are suddenly seen in a hard, clear
Northern light. One solitary bird moves among them on
the "shingle shelf" of the raised beach. The theme—it
dawns on one—has been stated in the opening line: "All is

lithogenesis—or lochia." And it is only the former that matters from the poet's point of view here. Lithogenesis, the creation or "birth" of the stones, the first product of the womb of the cosmos, is all-important in comparison with anything that has followed it in the "lochia," the evacuations from the womb after birth. That is the definition of "lochia" given in the English dictionary known to have been much used by MacDiarmid, and in his view these messy evacuations include such "superficial by-products" as the varieties of organic life and ultimately human civilisation itself. The poet's mind seeks to extricate itself from all that and to enter the timeless moment in which potential creation stands poised eternally:

> It is reality that is at stake.
> Being and non-being with equal weapons here
> Confront each other for it.. . .

All human knowledge is confounded by

> the ordered adjustments
> Out of reach of perceptive understanding
> Forever taking place on the Earth and in the
>   unthinkable regions around it.

Our only clue is in the stones, which are "one with the stars"—and we are told:

> No visitor comes from the stars
> But is the same as they are.

Of all things on Earth, only the stones are informed with the original "stupendous unity,"

> Always at the pitch of its powers,
> The foundation and end of all life.

We must concentrate our powers in a supreme effort to tune in to the "intense vibration in the stones/That makes them seem immobile to us," because

All else in the world cancels out, equal, capable
Of being replaced by other things . . .
But the world cannot dispense with the stones.
They alone are not redundant. Nothing can
    replace them
Except a new creation of God.   (426.)

About the poet himself, this now officially Marxist
materialist, we are told that his disposition is "towards
spiritual issues/Made inhumanly clear." (As he more
than once pointed out, following T. H. Huxley, 'matter' is
just a name for something we know very little about.) He
now demands of himself an immense inner concentration
like that of the stones. The sole nutriment his mind
hungers for is "bread from stones," to be perceived only in
"the deadly clarity of this 'seeing of a hungry man' " (an
echo of Doughty in *Arabia Deserta*). And, amongst the
imagery he continues indefatigably to find for the "barren
but beautiful reality" of this bleak world, there emerges
one image that has long haunted him. His inhuman,
abrasive concentration of the mind is aimed at stripping
away all the accretions of human culture, so as to be able
to "read the words cut oot i' the stane." The word for the
beginning and end of creation—and so its "meaning"—is
inscribed in the stones themselves:

   . . . the beginning and end of the world,
   The unsearchable masterpiece, the music of the
   spheres,
   Alpha and Omega, the Omnific Word.   (428–9.)

Stones as symbols of the end (as of the beginning)
inevitably conjure up tombstones to him, and in particular the stone that moved from Christ's tomb, "the
Christophanic rock." Thus the poem is also concerned
with MacDiarmid's acceptance of death, together with
what may come towards the close as a surprising hint of
eventual resurrection: "slow as the stones the powers

develop/To rise from the grave." One might have
expected, from the train of thought, something along the
lines of Yeats's speculation that perhaps "being is only
possessed by the dead," since organic life is Becoming, not
Being. There is also a reference to the human "betrayal"
of the stones which suggests, even at this late date, Solovy-
ovan ideas about the "duty" of human consciousness
towards the inanimate world, and consequently a conception of the evolutionary process and the value of human
culture fundamentally at variance with that adopted by
MacDiarmid in the rest of the poem. But few readers will
have been bothered by that. What is more likely to trouble
the reader is perhaps the question of how the "superficial
by-products" of organic life, as described by the poet,
could produce a specimen like him, capable of seeing
through them all to the "inoppugnable reality."

Consistency of *style* is, however, another matter, and
one that has more importance for the quality of the poem
as such. In that respect, MacDiarmid is more successful
here than in most of his long English poems. The more
ponderous passages, which one often feels to be reflecting
the style of his reading-matter, are not excessive in this
poem—though "the beauty of a maiden's cheek" is a bit
much for 1934—and there is a sense in which their very
ponderousness is appropriate to the poem. He can pare
his style down when he wants to, and he sustains a
brusque resilience, hammering away at the points of his
argument in aggressive fashion, but wielding the hammer
also with eloquent flourishes:

> There are plenty of ruined buildings in the
>   world but no ruined stones . . . .
> This is no heap of broken images. . . .
> These stones go through Man, straight to God,
>   if there is one.
> What have they not gone through already?
> Empires, civilisations, aeons. Only in them

If in anything can His creation confront Him.
They came so far out of the water and halted
    forever.
That larking dallier, the sun, has only been
    able to play
With superficial by-products since;
The moon moves the waters backwards and forwards,
But the stones cannot be lured an inch further
Either on this side of eternity or the other.
Who thinks God is easier to know than they are?
Trying to reach men any more, any otherwise, than
    they are?   (425, 427.)

There is also, unexpectedly, a socio-political dimension
to the poem, which, despite the awkwardness of some of its
implications, MacDiarmid handles with considerable
skill. It is first suggested near the beginning, by the statement that, just as the stones are indifferent to "all but all of
evolution," so "the essential life of mankind in the mass/Is
the same as their earliest ancestors' yet." Then, near the
end, he highlights it dramatically by saying that the bare
stone he grasps in his hand brings him to see

                            as before I never saw
The empty hand of my brother man,
The humanity no culture has reached, the mob.
Intelligentsia, our impossible and imperative job!

At the very end, he returns to his recondite vocabulary,
which though still very densely packed, may now be seen
to have more to offer the reader. Or at least the patient
reader, who is willing to penetrate the hard words as the
poet has striven to penetrate the stones. He will find that
diallage is "a figure of speech by which arguments, after
being considered from various points of view, are all
brought to bear on one point"—*and*, with a change of
pronunciation, it is a mineral which exhibits a play of

colour. Thus, in a great Joycean pun, it becomes a metaphor for the entire poem, in which, whatever the facets of the argument, "they all come back to the likeness of stone." And the last word in the poem, *epanadiplosis*, means "a figure by which a sentence begins and ends with the same word." Hence the stones, at the beginning and end of creation, are said to make "Earth's vast epanadiplosis."

Although there are scientific references in "On A Raised Beach," science provides background and reference-points rather than participating actively in the poem—and if it did, it would hardly be good science to claim that stones or rocks do not move. But without some geological knowledge MacDiarmid would not approach the stones in the way he does, and this knowledge contributes to their aptness as "objective correlatives" for some of the cold, bleak contents of his mind at this stage in his career. He makes little use, however, of what might seem the most promising aspect of science for his poetry: science as a fresh source of metaphor, of imagery. The image, at the end of "On A Raised Beach," of song as an apprentice encrinite (fossil sea-lily) is less effective than simply calling the living "the apprentice deid," as he had done in *Cencrastus*. It smacks too much of the strained ingenuities of "metaphysical" wit.

Back in 1932, he had gone to zoology as a source of imagery, and made good use of the image of the water-beetle, *Dytiscus*:

> The problem in the pool is plain.
> Must men to higher things ascend
> For air like the Dytiscus there,
> Breathe through their spiracles, and turn
> To diving bells and seek their share
> Of sustenance in the slime again
> Till they clear life, as he his pool
> To starve in purity, the fool,

Their finished faculties mirrored, fegs,
Foiled-fierce as his three pairs of legs?
Praise be Dytiscus-men are rare.
Life's pool still foul and full of fare.
Long till to suicidal success attain
We water-beetles of the brain! (354.)

"Suicidal" because, if such men as the poet do ascend to "higher things," they will cease to be human, and the human animal will presumably be superseded.

There is very little as effective, or as human, as that use of analogy in the *Stony Limits* collection, and only one comparable example in the *Second Hymn to Lenin and Other Poems*, where he uses the tiny, single-celled creatures called foraminifera, whose shells pile up in unimaginable numbers on the ocean floor, to count the cost of evolving "genius:"

Now more and more on my concern with the
    lifted waves of genius gaining
I am aware of the lightless depths that
    beneath them lie;
And as one who hears their tiny shells
    incessantly raining
On the ocean floor as the foraminifera die. (535.)

The *Second Hymn* volume looks like an interim collection, with its Englished versions of parts of the "Ode," other pieces showing similar psychological interests, and a further group in which (as F. R. Leavis noticed) there are signs of Lawrence and Yeats. Some are admirable poems, technically as competent as anything he turned his hand to, but this volume shares with *Stony Limits* a number of pieces which come as a rude shock in the standard of workmanship the poet now thinks acceptable in his books. About a dozen of them can only be described as crude doggerel. It would have been one thing if he had offered specimens of competent journalistic verse along with his more durable wares, but this is quite another matter. A reader encountering MacDidarmid's poetry for the first time in these two volumes would surely conclude that the author was quite unaware of the painful crudeness and incompetence of some of his work.

There is no need to pick on the worst examples. It is enough to ask oneself how a poet who had shown such abundant evidence of his ear for rhythm, and his instinct for the word or phrase that would pull its full weight in the line of verse, could offer for serious consideration a level of writing which is fairly represented by this:

> The fools who say men must still bear any yoke
> Have no gifts, save cruelty, more than most
> other folk.   (395.)

And he could write at that level in the most deadly earnest, offering to the memory of his great hero, the Communist martyr John Maclean, lines so bad that, for any competent reader of poetry, they make a mockery of his intentions by ruining his poem.

But what were, ultimately, his intentions in writing these poems? As at certain points of frustration with *Cencrastus* a few years before, one feels that what he is producing is perhaps the deliberate anti-poetry of a man who has turned (or had to turn) his back on the "mere beauty" of the lyrical. And one may suspect that it is because he has lost something that he now so undervalues it, and tries to invest his remaining capital elsewhere.

Perhaps two poems in the *Second Hymn* volume can be used as straws in the wind here. In "The Covenanters," the poet's characteristic and inveterate opposition to all fixed opinions, dogmas, or creeds, is completely swept away by the appeal of a puritan fanaticism:

> The waves of their purposefulness go flooding
> through me.

This religion is simple, naked. Its values
  stand out
In black and white.. . . .
Its very ugliness is compelling,
Its bleakness uplifting.
It holds me in a fastness of security.   (551.)

And "Poetry and Propaganda," which is itself, significantly, a very poor specimen of poetry, ends as follows:

In short, any utterance that is not pure
Propaganda is impure propaganda for sure.   (558.)

Now, it is arguable that all art is propaganda, but some
specimens of this propaganda are better art than others.
And there are further distinctions that have to be made.
For example, it may be agreed that Coleridge's "Ancient
Mariner" is propaganda, but it is not propaganda on
behalf of a Society for the Prevention of Cruelty to
Albatrosses.

The objection to some of the poems in *Stony Limits* and
the *Second Hymn* is not that they are propaganda as such
but rather that they are badly written and crude. Even as
propaganda, they are grossly oversimplified in their
message. They tell us only about Bad Guys and Good
Guys; their values "stand out in black and white" precisely because they are crudely conceived; and they do not
utilise more than the barest fraction of the talents of the
man who wrote them.

Most of the propaganda is Douglasite, and one must
have much sympathy for a man who, living in conditions
of acute hardship for his family and himself, and keenly
aware of the economic miseries of his country, is yet convinced that for mankind "the struggle for material
existence is over. It has been won."[10] But poems either
good or bad may be written out of such a situation, and
poems such as "The Belly-Grip" are bad poems—and all
the more so because they may occasionally have good lines
in them, as is the case with "Genethliacon," for example.

There is an obvious contrast between the poems that were written out of a sense of the particularity of the individual words—MacDiarmid like Doughty writing his poetry "word by word"—and these examples where words are thrown in by the armful. Pretty well any words in any tolerable order will do for most of the time, so long as the main message gets across: the message which in itself is relied upon to give purpose, commitment, and significance to the whole business of writing. But the propaganda verse has at least one thing in common with the extreme experiments with synthetic or scientific English, which use words screened from our emotions as if to build what Saurat called the Third Convention, "where men can think without first having to feel." Where poetry is concerned, feeling is the touchstone of rhythm, and rhythm is related to the sense of form. At the same time as he excludes ordinary human feelings from his poems, or abstracts them all under the Social Credit banner, the poet is liable to become erratic in his sense of rhythm and form. Naturally, syntax is affected as well, especially in the poems that retain rhyme but show little concern about the price rhyme is exacting by way of syntactical contortions, fill-up phrases, and mere tags like "I wis" (to rhyme with "is").

In one way or another, signs are not wanting of the ever-increasing strain on the poet in what he must have felt at that time as most painful isolation and misappreciation, however brave a front he kept up by that mind-chilling exercise of sheer will which he was constantly pushing to breaking-point:

> . . . immense exercise of will,
> Inconceivable discipline, courage, and endurance,
> Self-purification and anti-humanity.　　(429.)

One cannot think it came as a surprise when he broke down physically and mentally in 1935.

According to his doctor, MacDiarmid's illness was due

to "a summation of numerous subconscious 'insults' arising from domestic difficulties a few years previously."[11] After a short spell in hospital, he returned to Shetland and prepared for a fresh start. But certain basic commitments appear already to have been made, including the choice of language. There is a poem called "The Point of Honour" which suggests more than any other, I think, the nature of the change involved in that choice.

In this poem, he revisits in his imagination the river Esk, whose rhythms had pulsed through his boyhood, and which he had celebrated in the Scots verse of "Water Music" and "Scots Unbound." Now, in spite of his subject, he turns to English. There are several echoes of Hopkins in the poem—he has obviously been reading Herbert Read on that poet, and has also picked up a reference of his to Emerson—and there are lines imitative of Hopkins in technique:

> Delights of dazzle and dare revealed
> In instant inscapes of fresh variation. . . .   (388.)

> Nay, gaily, daily, over abysses more ghastly
> Men cast spider-webs of creation.   (390.)

There are also echoes of various remarks made by the Russian critic D. S. Mirsky about Ivanov and about Yazykov, whose poems (said Mirsky, following Pushkin) are "cold and seething like champagne, . . . vivid and impulsive in their own crystalline splendour." But MacDiarmid feels he must now eschew "purely verbal magnificences" like those of Yazykov, and his imitation of Hopkins is to be a last fling at ringing the sound-changes. The quotation from Emerson he smuggles into his verse runs more fully as follows: "It is not metres, but a metre-making argument, that makes a poem—a thought so passionate and alive, that, like the spirit of a plant or an animal, it has an architecture of its own, and adorns nature with a new thing."

It is thought, intellectual power, of that intensity that MacDiarmid feels he must now rise to. But he has reached a major crisis in his art, and still lacks "the right temper which goes to the point of the terrible; the terrible crystal." He is quoting now from R. W. Dixon's letter about the "terrible pathos" he found in Hopkin's poetry—and it is highly ironic that when, years later, MacDiarmid again quoted the phrase, it was to say: "It is only in the Scots language I can achieve or maintain . . . 'the terrible crystal'; its sounds . . . bring me fully alive."[12]

At the end of the poem he is no nearer to unlocking that power of thought in himself, which is also the secret of the Esk, the river for which he felt such empathy in his boyhood. He is like the fish that appear stranded on the shingle of the river:

Stranded. I with them! Would I wish to bend her
   To me as she veers on her way again
Vivid and impulsive in crystalline splendour
   Cold and seething champagne?
No. So life leaves us. Already gleam
In the eyes of the young the flicker, the change,
The free enthusiasm that carries the stream
Suddenly out of my range.

The concluding note of apparent pessimism is very unusual in MacDiarmid. Evidently he was searching for some fresh impetus that would orientate him creatively as he turned from Scots to English, and the sporadic imitation of Hopkins is one of the indications that he has lost the place in the story of his own development. Of one thing he is certain, however:

No more of mere sound, the least part.

The move from Scots to English is a move away from "sound" in poetry, and all the associations which must adhere to that, in the case of a poet whose sensitivity to it

was crucial for the artistry of his previous poetry. Sound
has suddenly become "the least part" of the matter. Now
it is

> The intellectual flame's survival I sing.

And as he turns his back on "mere" sound in his poetry,
he says:

> I know how it acts, connecting words, implying
> A rate of movement, onomatopoeic art,
> Or making a reader start trying
> To interpret the mouth's actual movement
> As a gesture; or acting directly
> Like a tune—a mode that is different
> From the rest as darkness from light to me,
> These intelligible, this a mystery.
> Is not consciousness of a sound an act
> Of belief in it; are not movements of muscles
> Transferred, apprehended, as rhythms, or fact
> Of nature some other sense claims?

And thus, with appalling effrontery, he breaks off his old
affair with sound in a passage which is a rhymed adaptation, at second hand, of a book review. And the book was
called *Sound and Meaning in English Poetry*!

This raises a sensitive matter. As any reader at all
familiar with his work must know, MacDiarmid
appropriated choice samples of his reading for use in his
writing, in verse as in prose, throughout his career.
"We're all full of quotations," he said, "only some of us
are adroit enough to choose our quotations from sources
that aren't so easily checked as others." Moreover, being
an extremist in all things, he carried this practice further
than any other poet known to me. His attitude was that, if
what attracted him in a passage was not merely what was
said but the way of saying it, then he helped himself to the
latter.

It was not one of his enemies but a most loyal friend and admirer, Norman MacCaig, who remarked of him that he "despised scruples"—which is perhaps a polite way of saying that he was unscrupulous in such matters. And instances of this have so shocked some people that, having denounced them, they take the view that there is then no more to be said.

I do not share that view. It seems to me that any given instance of MacDiarmid's practice in this respect may, or may not, be worth the reader's attention on at least three counts. Firstly, the passage he has lifted from another writer may be of interest in itself, for any number of reasons. Secondly, he may see in what was written something quite different from that which the author saw, and this may prove to be illuminating in a different way. And thirdly, he may use the "found" material skilfully and interestingly for his own purposes in the writing of a poem—and clearly there may be considerable artistic value in this activity itself, aside from any credit that may be due for the ability to spot such material and how it might be used.

There was a great fuss in the columns of the *Times Literary Supplement*[13] in 1965, when Glyn Jones wrote in to report that MacDiarmid had lifted some words of his from a short story and made all but the first line of his poem, "Perfect," with these words, practically unaltered. But, whatever the offence to morality or legality, "Perfect" is in fact a good example of how such material can be presented in a fresh and valuable way, without even altering the words.

Perfect

On the Western Seaboard of South Uist

(Los muertos abren los ojos a los que viven)

I found a pigeon's skull on the machair,
All the bones pure white and dry, and chalky,
But perfect,
Without a crack or a flaw anywhere.

At the back, rising out of the beak,
Were twin domes like bubbles of thin bone
Almost transparent, where the brain had been
That fixed the tilt of the wings.   (573.)

One might say that MacDiarmid treats the image preserved in Jones's admirable words like a "found" object.
But he does not see in the image what Jones saw in it. The
perfection of the skull, emphasised by MacDiarmid's title
and his featuring of the word "perfect" in the notably
short third line of the poem, is not of particular
significance to Jones. In the short story, the skull (which is
that of a seagull, not a pigeon) is a symbol in the arcane
sense, being used ambiguously along with many other
such symbols in an ambience of dreams. But in the poem,
the natural object which is the bird's skull, objectively and
precisely described as though for its own sake, functions of
its own accord as symbol. The reader who is brought to
see, to really see, the tiny, fragile-seeming bubbles of bone
in which the brain had been which controlled all the
intricacies of the bird's flight, is looking at a symbol of
life's mystery. Thus, as presented by the poet, the image is
a fine example of what Ezra Pound and the Imagists
meant when they said "the proper and perfect symbol is
the natural object" itself.

There is also something of interest in the way in which
the words are organised in the form of the poem. This for
me is much less a matter of typography than of the pattern
of sounds which the typographical letters represent. The
sounds in all but the first line are ostensibly the same as on
the page of the short story, of course, but their pattern is
modified in the poem, and our awareness of their inter-
relationship is significantly enhanced.

The distribution of the words on the page may seem a
trivial matter, but in fact the patterning of the sounds
makes a positive contribution to the meaningful
experience of the reader. After the first stanza, which

conveys the perfect state of the skull as a whole, we zero in
on two tiny matching spheres of bone: *twin domes*. Now,
consider the relationship in sound between *twin domes* and
thin bone in the same line, pairing *twin* with *thin* and *dome(s)*
with *bone*, so as seemingly to articulate or enact in terms of
sound the meaning of what is being said. We are told they
are like *bubbles*, the sound of which may alert one's ear to
the surrounding alliteration. And so to the two pairs in
strict consonance—that is, their consonantal skeletons are
identical, but not their vowels: *back, beak; bone, been*.

And then the last line: important of course because it
carries the pay-load, but also because the mention of the
missing brain has introduced a new and *vital* element
which this final line has to suggest. Appropriately, then,
we get in it a different kind of sound-effect, with the vowel,
and not the consonantal structure, being repeated. And
the resonance of the ending is brought out by a rhythmical
effect: a momentary tightening up and releasing of
rhythm that affects us here like a scannable metre:

> That fíxed/the tílt/of the wíngs.

Finally, one has to consider the new context which
MacDiarmid supplies for the found object: a context built
up from the title, the epigraph, the change of locale, the
change of bird from gull to pigeon. The Spanish epigraph,
in its original form in *La Celestina*, would normally be translated as "the dead open the eyes of those who live,"
though in the version used here it could be the dead whose
eyes are opened: perhaps they watch the living. Though
Spanish, the epigraph has a Scottish connection for
readers who know that MacDiarmid's friend
Cunninghame Graham had it inscribed on his wife's
memorial stone. But the specific Scottish context is
established by the poet's choice of locale, "On the
Western Seaboard of South Uist," and his use in the first
line of the Gaelic word *machair* (low-lying beach, links).
For a reader familiar with MacDiarmid's work, the Celtic

associations are strengthened by recollections of what he wrote elsewhere about South Uist (for example, in the *Islands of Scotland*, where this poem first appeared), and of another pigeon, the rock-pigeon in his poem "Dìreadh III". These hang together round a common theme, the theme associated with the rock-pigeon and also the bird in "Lines for a Gaelic University"—that is, the spirit of Celtic Scotland:

> The Gaelic genius that is in this modern world . . .
> Seldom and shining as poetry itself.   (1191–2.)

And the principal connection with South Uist lies in the fact that it was there that Clanranald had his piper, his harper, and his bard, who was of that family, the MacMhuirichs, who supplied the last of all the hereditary Gaelic bards after upwards of fifteen generations in office. That may seem dead history, as dead as the pigeon's skull. But the associations of the bird with poetry—its flight "the poetry of motion"—and its further associations with what MacDiarmid conceived to be the Celtic spiritual *homeland*, these are familiar enough in his work for the reader to take them up here without undue strain if he wants to. In the book where the poem first appeared, he touches on just such matters as I have mentioned.

It was to these matters also that MacDiarmid returned, after his illness, when he began to pick up the pieces again. One very large piece, in particular, seemed to show the shape of things to come: "Lament for the Great Music." If all art was propaganda, this was propaganda for a return to the values of that Celtic world in which the skills of music and poetry were respected and used as a living part of the people's heritage.

REFERENCES

1. "Author's Note," *Drunk Man* (1953), p. x.
2. See, e.g., *F.M.*, 31 Mar. 1934, p. 7.
3. *S.C.*, Oct. 1922, p. 62.
4. "Aims and Opinions," B.B.C. Third Programme, 9 Mar. 1960.
5. *Literary Essays of Ezra Pound*, ed. T. S. Eliot, London 1954, p. 25.
6. *The Spirit of Language in Civilization*, London 1932, p. 172.
7. R. McQuillan has noted that MacDiarmid made much use of Chambers's *Twentieth Century Dictionary*. See "MacDiarmid's Other Dictionary," *Lines Review*, Sep. 1978, pp. 5–14.

8. *A.*, p. 189.

9. H. Keyserling, *Travel Diary*, London 1925, I, 171.

10. "Lament for the Great Music," 478.

11. D. Orr, "MacDiarmid—The Man," *Jabberwock*, 5, 1958, p. 15.

12. *L.P.*, p. 35.

13. Correspondence, 7 Jan.–13 May 1965. (Full details are recorded in the *Annual Bibliography of English Language and Literature*, not usually so informative about this author.)

CHAPTER VI

THE KIND OF POET YOU'VE GOT

When he started once more to plan for the poetry yet to come, MacDiarmid does not seem to have felt the need of a new aim as such. One might say rather that he reverted to unfinished business, taking up the challenge *Cencrastus* had failed to meet years before: the "creation of major forms" through a revival of the Celtic ethos. This implied at least the possibility of poetry on an epic scale, and in this respect he found welcome support in Charles Doughty.

His habit of coupling Doughty's name with that of the great experimenter Hopkins has sometimes given the impression that it was Doughty's linguistic experiments, his "synthetic Anglo-Saxon," that mainly attracted MacDiarmid to him. And it is true that he recognised a kindred spirit there: above all in what has been called Doughty's "radical feeling for the unit of speech, his concrete apprehension—his thing-sense—of the isolated word."[1] But MacDiarmid already possessed that—and made better use of it than Doughty ever did. For him, the deeper significance of Doughty's example lay in the fact of the English poet's having kept his eye firmly on East *and* West, and in his having taken as the subject of epic verse "the ancient British history," that is, the history of Celtic Britain . He had attempted (and, MacDiarmid thought, at least partially achieved), in the "heroic poetry" of *The Dawn in Britain*, what George Buchanan, Milton, Blake, and Matthew Arnold had all contemplated but, for various reasons, failed to do.

Now, nothing less than epic was big enough for

MacDiarmid to envisage when he returned to the fray, and he seems to have taken his long "Lament for the Great Music" as a starting-point. For all its length, it would be just a preliminary sample of his own kind of "heroic poetry," in which he would proceed to explore all the ramifications of the Gaelic Idea on an epic scale. At all events, the "Lament" provided a high and long-sustained note on which to sound his theme.

Ceòl Mór, the great classical music of the Highland bagpipe, had been suppressed along with so many other traditions of the Gaels in the long aftermath of 1745. But for MacDiarmid, this austere music, so characteristic of Highland Scotland and yet with Eastern affiliations, remained the crowning glory of Celtic civilisation. He sees it in the poem as embodying the essence of real civilisation, a way of life in which the artistic expression of spiritual and intellectual values was of prime concern, so that to hear one of the MacCrimmons, the hereditary pipers whose mastery of pibroch was held to have died with them, would be to

> have one glimpse of my beloved Scotland yet
> As the land I have dreamt of where the supreme
>   values
> Which the people recognise are states of mind
> Their ruling passion the attainment of higher
>   consciousness. . . .   (481.)

And his dream is that such a way of life may be fully realisable in the future, because the genius of Douglas has shown how the masses can be freed from economic tyranny, making it possible eventually for a high culture to spring from the people, and not merely from "privileged centres" as before. No doubt he would have said this is a mere matter of semantics, but the only word to describe the kind of value he sees in culture is "spiritual:" "Our spirit is of a being indestructible . . . The supreme reality is visible to the mind alone." Culture is essentially a matter of the enlargement of human consciousness in the spiritual evolution of what he calls "cosmic consciousness."

There is little change in the metaphysical bent of MacDiarmid's mind, or in his aim: it is the technique that is different, in the "Lament" and the work that followed it. Even "On A Raised Beach" retained such traditional apparatus as rhyme in some parts—not always effectively —but now rhyme is abandoned along with anything that could be called metrical regularity. Basically, it is the capitalised line-division that distinguishes this sort of verse from prose; but in addition to that there is quite often a degree of rhythmical organisation which is above that which the ear associates with prose. It is not just a matter of "chopped-up prose." But what my ear at any rate tells me is that MacDiarmid is manipulating sizable passages of prose throughout the "Lament." In some instances, of course, this can be shown factually to be the case: for example, in the material he has taken from an address by Norman Maclean, delivered at the unveiling of the memorials to the MacCrimmons on Skye in August 1933. But, in the philosophical, "theological," and historical parts of the poem also, one is aware of material from prose contexts being employed, along with occasional pieces of borrowed verse, including a fine passage already used in *Cencrastus*, the crux of which is as follows:

> The mind creates only to destroy;
> Amid the desolation language rises, and towers
> Above the ruins; and with language, music.   (474.)

As with many writers whose minds are habitually saturated in print, MacDiarmid's thinking proceeds from one recollection of his reading to another, with a considerable part of the interest stemming from the unexpectedness of the connections he makes, or suggests, between them. This is in essence the method by which a very long poem such as the "Lament" was written—and it seems to me that, having lowered the fence between prose and verse, he lets the poem run for too long. That may have a certain appropriateness, if one feels, as I do, that some of the pibrochs themselves run on too long (and there is no reason to let a tone-deaf poet bully one on that point). But the excessive length is a great pity, as the "Lament" has some deeply moving passages, and its heroic elegiac note is sustained in its stronger parts by MacDiarmid's sense of the immense loss which the wilful destruction of such Gaelic traditions involved—"seven years of a man's life and seven generations of pipers before him, to make a perfect piper"—and the lonely immensity of the task he has set himself in trying to restore them to imaginative life.

About the epic work in which he intended to continue and complete this task, extending his range to take in the whole Celtic world, little enough can be known with certainty, since he never carried it out. The title for the entire work was to be the same as that given to what was envisaged as its opening section, "Cornish Heroic Song for Valda Trevlyn," written in 1936. This, an elaborate intertwining of curious lore—"moniliform in my verses here"—to offer as a necklace for his Cornish wife, seems rather more complete in itself than most of his later poems; but it does suggest, in one of its innumerable parentheses, what may have been conceived as a major theme for the epic itself:

The Celtic genius—Cornwall, Scotland, Ireland,
    Wales—
Is to the English Ascendancy, the hideous khaki
    Empire,
As the white whale is to the killer whale,
The white whale displaying in its buccal cavity

The heavy oily blood-rich tongue which is the
    killer's especial delight.
The killer slips his head into the behemoth's mouth
And rives away part after part of the tongue until
Nothing remains in the white whale's mouth but
    a cicatrised stump.
Yet to-day we laugh gailv and show our healthy
    red tongues,
Red rags to John Bull—the Celtic colour flaunting
    again
In a world where the ravening sub-fusc more and
    more
Prevails. We young Celts arise with quick tongues
    intact
Though our elders lie tongueless under the ocean
    of history . . .
The deepest blood-being of the white race crying
    to England
'Consummatum est! Your Imperial *Pequod* is sunk.'
                        (708–9.)

Thus, by one of these ingenious multiple allusions that
are his special delight, MacDiarmid appropriates D. H.
Lawrence's identification of the white whale, Moby Dick,
with "the deepest blood-being of the white race," and
makes of this a warning that, in more ways than one,
Britannia no longer rules the waves.

The quoted passage may suggest that there is an active
political dimension to his Pan-Celticism, which is indeed
the case, but there is little development in that direction,
either here or in the other poems that one may reasonably
suppose to have been intended to form parts of the total
"Heroic Song:" "Dìreadh," "Poems of the East-West
Synthesis," the poems in *The Islands of Scotland*, and some
of those in *Lucky Poet*. From his prose, it is quite clear that
his conception of the Gaelic Idea had changed: the need to
"polarise Russia effectively" was replaced with the

discovery of a common cause by the Celt and the Slav, in both of whom East and West were said to meet; and from this he was to proceed along Scottish Communist lines "à la John Maclean" to envisage "Workers' Republics in Scotland, Ireland, Wales, and Cornwall, . . . a sort of Celtic Union of Socialist Soviet Republics in the British Isles."[2] But politics is only one strand among many—and usually not the strongest one—in the poems. There are people who think otherwise, but they seem to me too ready to endorse some of MacDiarmid's statements and ignore others. Two of the latter are as follows:

> Remember, I speak
> Never of the representative individual man as man,
> But always of the artist as the great exception
> To the whole human order of things.
>
> ("Dìreadh I," 1172.)

And: "I am . . . interested only in a very subordinate way in the politics of Socialism as a political theory; my real concern with Socialism is as an artist's organised approach to the interdependencies of life."[3]

His powers of organisation as an artist seem to have been overtaxed by the "Heroic Song," however. Early in 1939, its total length was stated to have reached "some 60,000 lines," but there is no evidence that he found anything that he could have employed artistically to hold this huge mass of material together. We know from his other writings that the great idea obsessing him was the idea that, briefly, "the impetus to civilisation was an Ur-Gaelic initiative and that in the Gaelic genius lies the reconciliation of East and West."[4] Starting from such texts as *Six Thousand Years of Gaelic Grandeur Unveiled* (L. Albert's 1936 edition of Roger O'Connor's *Chronicles of Eri*) and L. A. Waddell's *British Edda* (1930), he strove to tap the mythopoeic potential of this idea through a return to the roots of civilisation. He saw the Celt and the Slav both as being "outside Europe," and in finding an

ultimate meeting-place for them in Communism he
thought of himself as creating the "East-West Synthesis"
from which he believed the "new beginning" must
develop—the new beginning that had first fired his
imagination in response to Spengler's *Decline of the West*, as
suggested in the first work signed by Hugh MacDiarmid
back in 1922. But nowhere in the poetry of his later period
does he show that he has managed to construct from this a
mythology that is functioning for his poetry to the extent
that, say, Blake's functioned for his, however difficult it
might be for the uninitiated reader to grasp. His new
Muse, Audh the Deepminded, is not much more coopera-
tive than Athikte had been when it comes to holding the
threads together in what the poet calls his "braid-
binding."

The materials for MacDiarmid's epic undoubtedly
accumulated in profusion, but what became of the epic?
As he struggled to conjure it into existence by sheer force
of will, the element of boasting and bluster that was
always part of his persona in print—a type of intellectual
machismo—begins to come uncomfortably close to
paranoia. In poems such as "The Kulturkampf" and
"The Poet as Prophet," for example, he invents a prepo-
tent persona ("The Man for whom Gaeldom is Waiting")
amongst whose superhuman accomplishments not the
least is that of supposedly having written that great work
which for us readers must unfortunately remain a matter
of epic wishful thinking.

But, as MacDiarmid himself pointed out, "It tak's a
man o' brains to be a paranoiac." Amongst the wreckage
of the scheme for the "Heroic Song" there are fragments of
undoubted value and interest: see, for example, the third
of the "Dìreadh" poems. The pity of it is that, in his determination to think big, the poet is all too seldom prepared
to give his smaller products a chance to make their virtues
felt to adequate effect on their own scale. An example of
this is "The Glen of Silence," which in its short, thirteen-

line form is one of the most powerful statements ever made about the tragedy of the Highland clearances. The poet elaborated upon these thirteen lines in another fifty which eventually dissipate most of the power—and it is the much inferior, long version of the poem which, in the interests of completeness, is given in the *Complete Poems*.

It is a significant fact that, in *A Kist of Whistles*, the only collection of "New Poems" (though some go back to 1922) which MacDiarmid published between 1935 and 1955, there is not one that satisfies the reader as a fully realised poem. In the meanwhile, he was endlessly embroiled with his epic schemes. In 1939, in addition to the 60,000 lines of the "Heroic Song," there was an epic work entitled *Mature Art* for which a prospectus was issued by Jack Kahane's Obelisk Press in Paris. MacDiarmid reported that Kahane's death and the outbreak of war prevented its publication, and in March 1940 an item in the *New Alliance* indicated that it ran to 20,000 lines and was then planned to be published by subscription. It never did appear, but subsequent work was described in terms of parts, or volumes, of *Mature Art* (or *A Vision of World Language*, as it was called later).

The first of an intended four volumes eventually appeared in 1955, obviously much reworked since its inception in the Thirties, and having acquired the title *In Memoriam James Joyce* in the interim. It offers a modest 6,000-odd lines of what MacDiarmid called his new "world view" poetry, but it is useful, I think, to relate it back almost to his earliest work, and in particular to those parts of *Annals of the Five Senses* in which he wrestled with the problem of how, as an artist, he could put to use even a small fraction of the stimulating material which his omnivorous reading habits, geared to modern mass media of communication, constantly supplied him with, and which his habits as an intellectual journalist constantly preserved: "There was so much to read that there was hardly time to think. How could he digest the marvellous,

the epoch-making truths, which every day put before him!
And the still more marvellous lies!"[5] And, of course, the
marvellous profusion of facts, the bits of information of all
sorts, together with the innumerable items of interest as
specimens of all the different kinds and manners of
writing, which his insatiably curious mind discovered and
with tireless energy stored away in the salt mines he must
have used for filing cabinets. There is a "world view" there
in the sense that the mind in question is very responsive to
a remarkably wide range of stimuli from the world of
information: the perspective which the mind can bring to
bear on the world is rather another matter.

To the first of his "Dìreadh" poems, MacDiarmid
prefixed the statement: "I turn from the poetry of beauty
to the poetry of wisdom—of 'wisdom,' that is to say, the
poetry of moral and intellectual problems, and the
emotions they generate." It would be much more accurate
to say that he turned to the poetry of information—and
the danger of confusing that with wisdom is suggested by
Eliot:

  Where is the wisdom we have lost in knowledge?
  Where is the knowledge we have lost in information?

But MacDiarmid himself settled readily enough for "a
poetry of fact," as he came to call it—doubtless because he
had encountered other quotations more to his purpose.
One that became a favourite with him was from
Whitman: "The true use for the imaginative faculty of
modern times is to give ultimate vivification to facts, to
science, and to common lives."

In *This Modern Poetry* (1935), Babette Deutsch made use
of that quotation, together with others from Thoreau,
Frost, and Marianne Moore, in a way which strongly
suggests that MacDiarmid's turning to "a poetry of fact"
was influenced by her book. Most suggestive is her quotation from Thoreau:

I have a commonplace book for facts and another for poetry, but I find it difficult always to preserve the vague distinctions which I had in mind, for the most interesting and beautiful facts are so much the more poetry, and that is their success. . . . I see that if my facts were sufficiently vital and significant—perhaps transmuted more into the substance of the human mind—I would need but one book of poetry to contain them all.

In *Lucky Poet*, when giving specimens of his unpublished verse, MacDiarmid follows a passage used later in *In Memoriam James Joyce* with some lines incorporating that quotation from Thoreau, and adds: "That is the point I have reached."[6] He thus implies that he has achieved in his poetry what Thoreau desired. But *In Memoriam James Joyce* confutes the claim on page after page where he is content to pile up factual items with no apparent regard to which facts might be "the most interesting or beautiful," or "sufficiently vital and significant—perhaps transmuted more into the substance of the human mind." Whatever Thoreau meant precisely by the latter, the essence of it must surely be that these facts would be imaginatively taken into the mind like the imagery more conventionally associated with poetry in his time. And it is up to the poet to make good use of them. When a fact is just a fact, its discovery in a book may have an emotional effect on us, but it is rarely if ever that we return to the book to re-experience the emotion, as we do when a fact has been made into good art. And it is emotion which is the common factor also in "the poetry of wisdom" and "the poetry of beauty" as indicated in the quotation above, where MacDiarmid made his other claim for the value of his new kind of verse. He can and does present certain facts in a way that affects the reader as Thoreau envisaged, from time to time. But he doesn't produce more than 6,000 lines of verse in that way. He does it by cataloguing masses of facts on a scale and with a density that the master-cataloguer Whitman himself might view with some apprehension.

The epic massiveness of *In Memoriam James Joyce* is obtained at the cost of a sense of discrimination. Take the use of what are in effect learned bibliographies, such as the lists of linguistic studies which the poet assembles around the dominant theme of the work, the theme of language itself, which is also the main link with Joyce. It becomes a question of acute uneasiness to the reader whether MacDiarmid is handling these pedantic compilations with even that degree of discrimination which registers the point at which they become comic. Any list of names may have the appeal of poetry at its most primitive level, but some names have more appeal than others, as the poet at last acknowledges, to the reader's grateful relief:

> Shirokogoroff's *Psychomental Complex of the Tungus*;
> (If that line is not great poetry in itself
> Then I don't know what poetry is!)   (793.)

It is only too rarely that his sense of humour is brought into play: a great loss in MacDiarmid, the worst of whose excesses have often been redeemed by that saving grace. And there is an important sense in which a Gargantuan work like *In Memoriam* is a game between the poet and the reader: not just a game in the humorous sense, of course, but a game that requires a sense of humour if it is to continue to be entertaining.

That is the more relevant because, for a poet who devoted most of his career to projects for extremely large-scale works, MacDiarmid had a notably weak sense of architectonics. The six parts of *In Memoriam* are lopsided and uninteresting from the point of view of their inter-relationship. And the working sense of form, from verse-paragraph to verse-paragraph, is often reduced to the barest minimum by a lust for the encyclopedic that insists on packing in every available reference. One remembers

the remark in *Annals*: "Indeed it was his chiefest difficulty
. . . to exclude, to condemn, to say No." Here, only the
crudest of linking-devices can encompass so much: "We
have of course studied thoroughly . . . And we are fully
aware of . . . And on to . . . We are familiar with . . . So
we have read . . . And we have read all that is to be read
on . . . ." The very boasting in such passages is aimed at
provoking the reader, if only by way of irritation (the game
getting out of hand), because the structural device itself is
patently incapable of sustaining his attention.

The scale of the work is arrived at mainly by the
accumulation of itemised detail, and sometimes by a
sentence structure which is again reminiscent of those
parts of the *Annals* where he packed one parenthesis inside
another, and so on. The usefulness of the latter in suggesting the movement of his mind—which typically sets out
along one path of memory only to be diverted into side-
openings in unexpected directions before completing the
trip—is undeniable, though it sometimes tends to split the
reader's head open as he waits with increasing anxiety for
a closing bracket that perhaps will never come—and then
where will he be?

Hopkins wrote a chorus for his unfinished play, *St.
Winefred's Well*, which begins as follows:

How to kéep—is there ány any, is there none such,
        nowhere known some, bow or brooch or braid or
        brace, láce, latch or catch or key to keep
Back beauty, keep it, beauty, beauty, beauty, . . .
        from vanishing away?[7]

MacDiarmid asks the same question of knowledge, not
beauty, and the extended parenthesis between the beginning and the end of his question is filled (by the epic page)
with *factual* charms against the powers of mortality. The
kind of poetry he wants is a poetry of fact. And as his mind
operates in a continuum of factual information, so he

wants his poetry to provide blocks of facts and whole housing-schemes of quotations. The man lived in a two-roomed cottage, but his mind required much more extensive accommodation.

But how to design it? MacDiarmid found an ingenious way round that question. Claiming that Wagner and Doughty "knew that we were coming to another of the quantitative—as against accentual—periods in culture," he went on to state:

> It is this question of quantity as against accent that distorts to most Scots the nature of our pibrochs of the great period. These knew no "bar." They were *timeless* music—hence their affiliation with plainsong, with the neuma. Barred music—accented music—finds its ultimate form in symphony. Unbarred music—quantity music—expresses itself in pattern-repetition; hence the idea that the Celt has no architectonic power, that his art is confined to niggling involutions and intricacies—yet the ultimate form here is not symphony; it is epic.[8]

Since we are coming or have come to a quantitative period in culture, and the Age of Communism requires an epic expression "in keeping with the great enterprise" (indeed, "it is epic—and no lesser form—that equates with the classless society"), so pattern-repetition, and not architectonic power, is what we ought to have. Presumably it is in some such terms that MacDiarmid would have defended the way in which *In Memoriam* is put together. But the method as used by him is sometimes so primitive that it grates painfully against the erudite sophistication of his material. And he carries the pattern-repetition of his facts, nomenclature, and foreign phrases to such lengths that he loses sight of the most important fact of all. That is, the fact that the number of items known as such is relatively of little importance to the function of art as he himself defined it—"the extension of human consciousness." What matters most in this respect is the extent to which items of knowledge can be *inter-related*.

We don't expect a poet to attempt this through logical systemisation, but we do expect him to make imaginative use of some process of analogy. And, in fact, MacDiarmid arrives at some of the best things in *In Memoriam*, as in his later poetry generally, by drawing upon scientific and other factual information for illuminating analogies. For example:

> (Silence supervening at poetry's height,
> Like the haemolytic streptococcus
> In the sore throat preceding rheumatic fever
> But which, at the height of the sickness,
> Is no longer there, but has been and gone!
> Or as 'laughter is the representative of tragedy
> When tragedy is away.')   (771.)

But such passages are few and far between, and being relatively short they tend to be swamped by the surrounding material. For the rest, it is largely a matter of each reader taking his pick amongst the curious lore which the poet produces from the caverns of memory or the recesses of his formidable filing-system. The poet will constantly press upon him much, much more than he could conceivably want, but there is also the prospect of some very rare collector's items.

It should be clear enough that the items so collected did not originate with the poet himself. This is a "poetry of fact," begun in the Thirties when writers of all kinds were seeing their function as essentially "documentary." It goes back in one direction to the Russian Futurists' insistence that their work was not to be considered as "purely aesthetic striving" but rather as a "laboratory" for the expression of facts. And in another direction it takes in Ezra Pound's "use *as a language* of multifarious references to all periods of history and all phases of human activity."[9] Together, these give a fair indication of what

MacDiarmid at any rate hoped to achieve by "documentation." However, in his habitual fashion, he pushes to an extreme the method of documentation by using passages from other people's writings, and this can be hard to take, particularly when he ignores the matter of copyright.

A case in point is the passage above, about the haemolytic streptococcus. No one cares where he got the bit of medical information from, since such material is regarded as common property. The short remark about laughter as the representative of tragedy is presumably all right because it has quotation marks round it. (As a matter of interest, it comes from Wyndham Lewis.) But this passage is interpolated in the poem at a point where there is a reference to Hölderlin, who "sought,/And often miraculously found,/The word with which silence speaks/Its own silence without breaking it." And Hölderlin is being contrasted with Karl Kraus, about whose relations with language we learn a great deal in the longest sustained stretch of this sort in the entire poem, running to about nine pages of text in the *Complete Poems*. And all that material has been taken from an unsigned article in the *Times Literary Supplement*, which is just identified in a footnote.[10]

This is stretching the notion of "documentation" a lot further than many people are prepared to follow him. Yet there is more to it than may at first appear. The commentary on Kraus is not only an outstandingly perceptive piece of writing, of great interest in its content; it is the work of a fine stylist with a very unusual feeling for rhythm.[11] And MacDiarmid brings out the rhythmical pattern of parts of the prose by cutting them into verse-lines:

> What was the inspiration of his vast
>   productivity?
> The answer is Hamlet's: "Words, words, words!",

And the commas between them
And the deeds they beget
And the deeds they leave undone;
And the word that was at the beginning,
And, above all, the words that were at the end.

(768.)

Anyone who looks closely at the little changes, including word-substitutions, that have been made in the original, will recognise that the hand of the poet has not lost its old cunning. And at least it is employed to better effect here than in the bulk of *In Memoriam*, where bits of linguistic and literary information are manipulated without such glaring offence to the guardians of copyright but with, alas, no comparable pleasure for the reader. As to the principle that scrupulous acknowledgment of quotations should be made, it is rather absurd to apply that to the sort of work that is, strictly speaking, little else but quotation from beginning to end, like the discourse of many literary people. And, *pace* writers of letters to the *T.L.S.*, it is hard to understand how anyone could actually read the poem without realising *that*. Nor is its method, though pushed to the extreme, a scandal for its time, the age of modernism. As Eduardo Paolozzi has said: "Modernism is the process where plagiarism and pastiche become indistinguishable."[12]

The reading of the poem itself involves an adjustment which I confess I do not find it easy to make. As David Daiches noted in a blindingly simple observation, the poem ought to be read *rapidly*, and that implies an attitude towards the language of poetry I am disposed to resist. Clearly, willingness to try out a different concept of poetry is required, and that is good for one. But if in the event one finds one is skimming and skipping to relieve one's boredom with the way the language is being used, one cannot very well regard that as other than a deplorable fact. Nor is it easy to accept the view that MacDiarmid in

his later work is, as a modernist, deliberately choosing to
do without the appeal of form and selection in order to
present the continuum in which the mind of modern man
actually exists, when he so often tells us in that very work
that what he wants above all is for it to be "organised to
the last degree:"

> Organize. Organize. Organize.
> Everything is a matter of organization,
> Not of primal substance.   ('Dìreadh I,' 1173.)

Of course, being MacDiarmid, he will also say the
opposite at times, but there is little doubt which side the
artist in him was on.

He was obsessed to the end with 'The Impossible
Song'—impossible to realise but not to envisage—that
should by some miracle express all the fantastic variety
and nimiety of the inner world a lifetime's reading
discovered for his mind to celebrate. For over twenty years
he assembled a sequence of samples, like charms that
might work the miracle—or, to revert to his early work
again, like the handout as a form of literature—called *The
Kind of Poetry I Want*, published in book form in 1961, as the
second volume of the work perpetually in progress. He
said then that "this is the first time all the pieces have been
brought together, set in their proper sequence, and
published as a single poem." That would imply that he
had rejected many of the pieces of *The Kind of Poetry I Want*
which had appeared earlier, including some of the better
specimens, and had radically changed the attitude that
led him to give complete freedom to the radio producer D.
G. Bridson in determining the choice and order of
passages for a broadcast of the work only a year before.[13]
But in reality the sequence was potentially endless, its
parts indefinitely permutable. He persisted in referring to
his work as "Song," though he knew "It is no song that
conveys the feeling/That there is no reason why it should
ever stop." It could be given form only in a very primitive

way: "Poetry that never for a moment forgets" such-and-such, "not unaware of" this and that, and "like" as many other things as possible, rather than just the most illuminating.

That is not to deny that the appeal of his charms and incantations can be strong, as indeed the intrinsic interest of some of them is great. At their best they can appeal simultaneously to the intelligence and the imagination:

> A poetry like the hope of achieving ere very
>   long
> A tolerable idea of what happens from first to
>   last
> If we bend a piece of wire
> Backwards and forwards until it breaks.   (1009.)

There are much more spectacular examples, too, of his ability to introduce into poetry material that had traditionally been regarded as foreign to its nature. And it is true that by unexpected juxtapositions he can sometimes play off individual items against each other effectively. Nevertheless, it is the desire to go on for ever, drawing on his inexhaustible store of "found" material—facts, descriptions, ideas—that compels him to present all this relentlessly as epic, rather than settling for something smaller that he is in practice better equipped to handle:

>   The kind of poetry I want
> Is poems *de longue haleine*—far too long
> To be practical for any existing medium. . . .   (608.)

Or existing reader, perhaps? Fit readers will only come in "the epical age of Communism," of which he sees himself as a "harbinger," when everyone will have followed the directive of Lenin and "worked over in his consciousness the whole inheritance of human knowledge,"[14] using a great deal more than the present average of two per cent or so of his brain cells.

In the meanwhile, in so far as he gets into print at all, the poet acts as a kind of sub-editor in an intellectual news agency, sorting out the items he finds of interest, sometimes underlining points where they converge, sometimes mixing them together unexpectedly to stimulate the reader's attention, and insisting throughout on doing away with what Chaim Bialik called "the folly of differentiating between prose and poetry." If this is a form of "documentary," it documents one man's insatiable and wide-ranging reading—more of book reviews than of books, it should be said, though it would be foolish to underestimate the latter, or take him at his word when he remarks that in this respect he is like Tom Mooney, who read the latest books "only in review."[15]

To sum up, his later work is mainly a product of what Coleridge meant by the Fancy, which, he said, "has no counters to play with but fixities and definites. The Fancy is . . . a mode of memory emancipated from the order of time and space, while it is blended with and modified by . . . Choice. But equally with the ordinary memory the Fancy must receive all its materials ready made from the law of association."[16] By that I do not mean, any more than Coleridge would, to condemn the work out of hand, but to indicate its basic limitation as I see it.

The projected third volume of the "work in progress" was finally abandoned when MacDiarmid's *Complete Poems* was prepared for publication. It remains for me only to mention *The Battle Continues*, an epic-scale example of *flyting*, a form of warfare by verbal abuse which is found in both the Lowland and the Highland Scots traditions. Although begun about 1939, this ferocious assault in the war of words between MacDiarmid and Franco's South African champion, Roy Campbell, did not reach print till 1957, by which time the other combatant had unfortunately left the scene of action.[17]

As parts of the *Complete Poems* will rapidly indicate to any reader, MacDiarmid wrote far too much, quoted far too much, discriminated far too little, and had too weak a sense of form for the mammoth projects he undertook. But he is, in my opinion, a poet of major stature: perhaps as big in his faults and failures as in his virtues and successes, but *big*. In the end he will stand by what he did best, and that is no small achievement.

> Surrendering and dispersing his identity
> He yet made the world feel him at last
> As something tough, something singular,
>   something leathery with life . . . .
> But there was one virtue the meanest
>   allotment-holders have
> Which he conspicuously lacked—they *weed* their
>   plots
> While he left to time and chance
> And the near-sighted pecking of critics
> The necessary paring and cutting.   (703, 702.)

REFERENCES

1. B. Fairley, "Introduction," *Selected Passages from "The Dawn in Britain" of Charles Doughty*, London 1935, pp. xvi–xvii.
2. *L.P.*, p. 26.
3. *L.P.*, p. 241.
4. *Golden Treasury of Scottish Poetry* (1946 edn.), p. xxiii.
5. *A.*, p. 110.
6. *L.P.*, p. 327.
7. *Poems*, ed. R. Bridges, London 1918, p. 54.
8. "Charles Doughty and the Need for Heroic Poetry" (1936). In *S.E.*, pp. 75–6.
9. *S.E.*, p. 80.
10. "Satirist in the Modern World," *T.L.S.*, 8 May 1953, pp. 293–95.
11. Hamish Henderson has identified the author as Erich Heller, whose unusual rhythmic sense may have been developed by writing in more than one language.
12. "Junk and the New Arts and Crafts Movement," *Cencrastus*, Autumn 1979, p. 6.
13. B.B.C. Third Programme, 14 March 1960.
14. Quoted, e.g., in *L.P.*, p. xxii.
15. *L.P.*, p. xvii.
16. *Biographia Literaria*, chpt. xiii.
17. For a brief attack by Campbell, see *The Author*, Summer 1955, pp. 92–3.

CHAPTER VII

REPUTATION

This account of the poet's literary reputation will inevitably centre on Scotland, where a thread of interest in Scots poetry can be traced with some degree of continuity throughout the period concerned. C. M. Grieve was already regarded there as the most promising poet of the younger generation, on the strength of his poems in English, when the possibility of a literary revival or "renaissance" was mooted in the early Twenties. And when the Scots poems of Hugh MacDiarmid began to appear, there were three people writing mainly for the *Glasgow Herald* who quickly recognised their exceptional qualities: William Power, Alexander McGill, and Robert Bain. They ensured, by their efforts in the *Herald* and elsewhere, that these poems and the aims of the short-lived periodicals in which they appeared were made known to a wider circle of readers.

When MacDiarmid's own periodicals had given up the unequal struggle, McGill saw another possibility of reaching potential readers by making use of the *Scottish Educational Journal*, a weekly read mainly by teachers. His article, "Towards A Scottish Renaissance,"[1] paved the way for MacDiarmid's highly provocative (and often critically acute) series, "Contemporary Scottish Studies," which began in June 1925 and led to much controversy in the columns of the *Journal*. By the time he published some of the articles in book form the following year, he had become notorious, and it should be noted that opposition to MacDiarmid as a writer was based more on these articles than upon his early experiments in Scots verse.

The latter were accepted and appreciated by a surprising number of readers, when one remembers the extent of the public for any kind of serious poetry, let alone experimental contemporary verse in the vernacular, which was quite as suspect a commodity to most Scotsmen as to Englishmen of the time.

Few enough copies of *Sangschaw* and *Penny Wheep* were sold, no doubt, but they did begin to establish a solid basis for MacDiarmid's reputation as a Scots poet, and he could certainly take comfort from the knowledge that those few readers whom he considered to possess decent critical standards thought very highly of them. No critic could in fairness be expected to come to terms with *A Drunk Man* immediately, though the poet's memory was at fault when he said it was reviewed "very unfavourably" in the *Glasgow Herald*, and Compton Mackenzie wrote of his first encounter with that work in 1927 that "it was as if a tremendous explosion had taken place to clear the air and reveal the sublime landscape which hitherto I had only perceived in a misty mid-region between sleep and wakefulness."[2]

MacDiarmid always delighted in the most outrageous sort of self-propaganda, and he carefully consolidated the notoriety he had achieved. *To Circumjack Cencrastus* (1930) was heralded by advance reviews written anonymously or pseudonymously by the poet himself in at least half a dozen different journals: "each a different article; quite a little journalistic feat!"[3] He was at pains to point out that *Cencrastus* contained outspoken attacks on "all manner of prominent Scottish personalities" and that "many of its passages would be characterised by any section of the Christian Church as blankly blasphemous."[4] Less predictably, he also criticised his own "gratuitous ill-will," "Ishmaelitism," "pretentious pendantry," "intellectual arrogance," and "cheap sarcasm" with almost as much gusto as he had shown in criticising other people's failings in the book itself.[5]

The result was that even his poetry made news in the Scottish press. The Glasgow *Daily Record* greeted the appearance of *Cencrastus* with what it called "a double-barrelled review by two prominent literary figures," the Rev. Dr. Lauchlan Maclean Watt (who was sideswiped in the poem on his way to becoming Moderator of the General Assembly of the Church of Scotland) and William Power.[6] Inflamed letters to the Editor followed.

MacDiarmid's fame as distinct from his notoriety grew quite steadily until the series of crises that took him to the Shetland Islands and away from the public arena. There is indeed what one might call an awe-inspiring example of the effect of his great potentiality on a reader in many ways antipathetic to what he stood for. W. H. Hamilton, for whose literary tastes and religious convictions MacDiarmid had little but scorn, nevertheless wrote of the author of *First Hymn to Lenin and Other Poems* (1931): "the conviction grows steadily that in him a very great poet has been born and is being painfully made, and that no small reverence becomes the critic in the presence of his gift."[7]

When the poet protested against a very unfavourable anonymous review of his next book of verse, *Scots Unbound*, in the same journal, which was edited by his friend Power, the reviewer roundly retorted that "there is no important Scottish writer to-day, critical or creative, but has praised MacDiarmid's poetry, and no other Scottish writer has received such attention or been discussed so much . . . . Martyrdom has eluded him. He is a successful poet."[8] But the successful poet, only a few months later, was struggling in exile against abject poverty and mental if not physical hardship, with his wife and their baby.

During the long years in Shetland MacDiarmid found himself debarred increasingly from appearing in the periodical press, by his own account largely for political reasons. Relatively little was heard of him as a poet, and the general assumption was that his vein of poetry had been more or less exhausted. In a contribution to *Edinburgh Essays in Scots Literature* (1933), Ian A. Gordon had already voiced the majority opinion by describing him as "the finest lyric poet in Scotland" but deploring his recent change to "a style that is inconsequent always, incoherent very often, and is all too seldom poetry."[9] *Stony Limits* (1934) and *Second Hymn to Lenin and Other Poems* (1935) posed problems the critics were not disposed to tackle, and were given little attention.

Then came the critical blow that MacDiarmid felt most keenly. Edwin Muir, a Scottish critic whose literary judgments could be expected to have some effect outside Scotland, had written the first important assessment of his work, a review of *Annals of the Five Senses* for the *New Age*. Some remarks about the un-Englishness of the author led to a comparison with James Joyce, and Muir gave it as his opinion that "except Mr. Joyce, nobody at present is writing more resourceful English prose."[10] In reviewing *Sangschaw* and introducing the new Scottish literary movement to American readers of the *Saturday Review of Literature*, he compared MacDiarmid very favourably with his English contemporaries; he admired *A Drunk Man*; and in a review of *Cencrastus* for Eliot's *Criterion*, after declaring that its author was "the most considerable Scottish poet since Burns," he stated that "a poem so long, so various, and so sustained at this, written on such a theme, could only have been written by a man of poetic genius."[11]

But by 1934 Muir was expressing grave doubts about the possibilities of Scots as a literary medium.[12] Then he seemed to have swallowed his doubts when in May 1935 he wrote that MacDiarmid "has done something for Scottish poetry of quite unique value; he has made it a vehicle capable of expressing, like English or French, the feelings and thoughts of the contemporary world."[13] A year later, however, he wrote an article for *Outlook* setting out his case against the use of Scots,[14] and this became a central point in his book, *Scott and Scotland* (1936). Remarking that Scotland has lacked a homogeneous language since the sixteenth century, he said that the predicament of the Scottish writer

> cannot be solved by writing poems in Scots, or by looking forward to some hypothetical Scotland in the future . . . . Scottish poetry exists in a vacuum . . . . Hugh MacDiarmid has recently tried to revive it by impregnating it with all the contemporary influences of Europe one after another, and thus galvanise it into life by a series of violent shocks. In carrying out this experiment he has written some remarkable poetry; but he has left Scottish verse very much where it was before.[15]

Splinters from the ensuing explosion are to be found in many of MacDiarmid's later writings. To adapt a celebrated MacDiarmidism, from being a man after Edwin Muir's heart he became a man after Edwin Muir's blood, and though Muir subsequently modified his views to some extent, the breach between them was never healed. It should be noted, however, that MacDiarmid was not here concerned directly with himself but with the implication that it would be a waste of time for other writers to continue the attempt at reviving Scots as a literary language.

When the War and its aftermath brought him back to Clydeside, a group of younger writers formed round him, most of them writing verse in Scots or Gaelic, for which they found an enthusiastic publisher in William Maclellan of Glasgow. MacDiarmid was for them a modern master of their craft, his work in Scots an achievement of the highest order, guaranteeing the reality of a national literary revival in which they could and would play their part. While there could be plenty of argument about this "second wave of the Scottish Renaissance," one fact was unequivocal: MacDiarmid's work was becoming a major force in contemporary Scottish writing. The tide was clearly against Muir, whose comments had meanwhile become more circumspect. Comparing MacDiarmid with his arch-enemy, Roy Campbell, he said: "Technically Campbell is by far the more accomplished poet, but MacDiarmid excells him in intelligence and in grotesque satirical fancy, half philosophical, half comic." And of *A Drunk Man* he observed that "technically it is uneven and often careless, but it contains brilliant passages, it is seldom flat, and it is the work of an interesting mind. MacDiarmid's later poetry, much of it Communistic, is poor by comparison and often dull."[16]

MacDiarmid's reputation then passed through a testing period in which it survived the inevitable reaction of a still younger generation against what seemed to some of them to be a pontifical grandfather-figure. Significant support for MacDiarmid came from three of the most accomplished poets whose own reputations were being established: Norman MacCaig, Sorley Maclean, and (later) Edwin Morgan. Although they differed greatly in their individual approaches to poetry, and admired and did otherwise where MacDiarmid's actual practice was concerned, they were unanimous in regarding him as one of the major poets of his time.

His later work, *In Memoriam James Joyce* and *The Kind of Poetry I Want*, gradually achieved at least one of MacDiarmid's aims: to stir up live literary controversy in Scotland. Its leading apologist, Edwin Morgan, set up a persuasive case for its importance, and my own view—that it proved to be largely a dead-end for MacDiarmid himself, however suggestive it may be to other writers who can take what they want and pass over the rest—is far from being unchallenged.

Morgan argued part of his brief for the later poetry in the *Festschrift* published in Edinburgh to celebrate MacDiarmid's seventieth birthday in August 1962. As might be expected of that form of publication, the

Festschrift had its ups and downs in quality, but it contained some excellent articles and showed how enormously stimulating the man and his work had been to
Scotsmen of different generations.

MacDiarmid's experiences in the Thirties had embit-
tered his subsequent relations with Scottish publishers,
and it was only after publication by Macmillan of New
York that the 1962 volume of his *Collected Poems* was issued
by Oliver and Boyd in Scotland. In the *Scotsman*, a national
newspaper which for many years had prosecuted a policy
of avoiding even the mention of MacDiarmid's name,
though more recently seeking to make amends, Andrew
Hood declared that "this collection shows conclusively
that he is a poet of the first rank," and "it is time that
Scotland, and not merely a few percipient Scots,
recognised his stature."[17] The only other review of note in
Scotland appeared in the *Glasgow Herald*, where Edwin
Morgan enquired when we would see English criticism
recognising the fact that "MacDiarmid has little to fear
from comparison with those who could be thought of as
his most distinguished contemporaries"—all, in
Morgan's view, American poets: Eliot, Pound, Williams,
Stevens.[18]

1964 saw the publication of my critical study of
MacDiarmid in the "Writers and Critics" series and a
survey of MacDiarmid and other writers associated with
the Scottish Renaissance by Duncan Glen.[19] It might be
agreed that these have proved useful to writers of subsequent criticism and academic dissertations on the poet, of
which there has been an evergrowing number. Glen is the
energetic editor of the magazine *Akros*, two double-issues
of which were devoted to the assessment of MacDiarmid
in 1970 and 1977. Other critical symposia have been
featured in magazines from *Agenda* (1967–68) to the
Scottish Literary Journal (1978). Many of the items available
in 1972 were reprinted in *Hugh MacDiarmid: A Critical
Survey*, edited by Glen, and readers may consult the Select

Bibliography below for some others of importance.

This short survey is concerned with MacDiarmid's *literary* reputation, though it is really impossible to isolate the strictly literary aspect of a man characterised by Compton Mackenzie nearly half a century ago as "the most powerful intellectually and emotionally fertilizing force Scotland has known since the death of Burns."[20] While they certainly indicate the fame he eventually achieved, one can scarcely measure the literary fall-out from such things as the birthday celebrations that punctuated his later years, the films made about him (some reaching a large audience through television), or the pictorial biography published by Gordon Wright in 1977. The inter-relationship between his work and the rise of Scottish Nationalism, an altogether deeper matter than the recorded history of political parties, will always be beyond calculation. It is not for nothing that the latest collection of essays on this writer and his influence in Scotland is called *The Age of MacDiarmid* (1980).

Outside Scotland, one finds sporadic bursts of interest in various countries, without much evidence that the recently accelerated awareness of MacDiarmid was based on appreciation of his writing rather than its being a by-product of the communications industry. One of the earliest admirers of his work was Denis Saurat, who introduced him to French readers in 1924, in an essay embodying translations of his poems, the finest of which he judged to be "The Watergaw," calling it "un véritable chef d'oeuvre . . . de simplicité et de concision essentielles. . . . Si beaucoup de poèmes de cette force nous sont révélés, le groupe de la *Renaissance écossaise* aura tenu sa gageure et conquis une place en Europe."[21] This was followed by an article in which Saurat stressed the point that MacDiarmid was potentially of European stature and in this respect should take the place of Burns: "Burns n'était européen que par ses platitudes."[22] Thirty years later, one of the few adventurous spirits who grappled with *In Memoriam James Joyce* was the French critic Michel Habart.[23]

MacDiarmid himself testified that the encouragement he received from Irish writers from Yeats to Sean O'Casey meant a great deal to him. George Russell ("AE") wrote an introduction to the *First Hymn to Lenin and Other Poems*, calling its author a poet of genius, and Oliver St. John Gogarty declared that *A Drunk Man* was "the most virile and vivid poetry written in English or any dialect thereof for many a long day."[24] The high point of *A Drunk Man* for Gogarty was the now famous lyric, "O Wha's Been Here Afore Me, Lass," which he showed to Yeats, with the result that the latter included it (with other poems by MacDiarmid) in his *Oxford Book of Modern English Verse.* Gogarty has said that Yeats at that time was "amazed that there should be such writing and he unaware of it."[25]

German studies include a general survey of "Die Schottische Renaissancebewegung" by Reinald Hoops (1933)[26] and an assessment dealing mainly with MacDiarmid by Rolf Blaeser (1958).[27] During the last three decades, considerable interest in his work has been shown in Russia, other Eastern European countries, and China. While this is politically activated as a matter of course, it is hardly likely that there should be much concern for a Scottish poet in those parts of the world if his poetry was not judged to be valuable as poetry. A bad or insignificant poet is not much of a political prize, particularly if he happens to be a nationalist deviationist. So far as the present writer is aware, the most substantial critical work on MacDiarmid in the Communist world is the well-informed study of his poetry by a Hungarian scholar, József Szili, in 1959,[28] described by John Wain as "some hogwash written by a Government hack in Budapest."[29] There have also been articles in Czechoslovakia (1951 and 1962), Poland (1956), and Russia (1967).[30] Poems by MacDiarmid have been translated into many languages.

In the United States, nothing of much interest appeared between Muir's review of *Sangschaw* in 1925 and Babette Deutsch's book *This Modern Poetry* in 1935. The first substantial, if critically underweight, consideration of MacDiarmid's work was an article in the *Sewanee Review* by James G. Southworth,[31] reprinted as a chapter of his book *Sowing The Spring* (1940). Though Southworth was sympathetic towards most of the poet's aims in so far as he understood them, and impressed by his powers as a thinker, the language difficulty loomed much larger than it need have done. It took a Scottish critic, David Daiches, writing in *Poetry* (Chicago),[32] to make the essential point that "MacDiarmid does not use Scots as an *alternative* to English; he uses it for effects which are *unobtainable* in English." However, an American who had no difficulty in seeing (and hearing) that MacDiarmid's use of Scots was "unmistakably vital" published an article in 1952, celebrating his discovery of a lyrical gift "which is, as in Blake and Burns, a form of genius." This was Charles Glicksberg,[33] who, though apt to choke on his indignation when confronted with MacDiarmid's Marxist propaganda, responded warmly to the vein of true poetry he found elsewhere in his work, and gave a perceptive critical account of it.

Another American critic, M. L. Rosenthal, had a sufficiently "sympathetic ear" for what he called "a half-foreign tongue" to discern that MacDiarmid's best work is in Scots.[34] But there were few enough hints of a potential American readership for the *Collected Poems*, which Macmillan of New York nevertheless published successfully in 1962. It was a far from satisfactory edition of the poems, but bringing it out at all seemed so much of a miracle that one could but echo Daiches' words in the *New York Times*: "Our gratitude goes out to Macmillan for producing this first collected edition of one of the very great poets of our time."[35] The success of the venture (there was a second, cosmetically revised edition in 1976) must have been due to no small number of readers sharing the experience of Carolyn Kizer, who reviewed the volume for *Poetry*.[36] Alternately enthralled and infuriated by her sudden exposure to MacDiarmid in full spate, she managed to convey a sense of the sheer delight his work offers at its best—and how many modern poets can give that sort of spontaneous pleasure?

English critics showed little interest in MacDiarmid for the forty years prior to the appearance of the *Collected Poems*. F. R. Leavis seemed to provide a rare exception to prove the rule when he said in 1935 that the "Second Hymn to Lenin" "is sufficiently a success to deserve inclusion in the ideal anthology (which would be a very small one) of contemporary poetry."[37] However, he did not explain why he thought this was so, and his track record as a judge of contemporary poetry was not very impressive. Cecil Day Lewis was interested in the "First Hymn to Lenin" from the viewpoint of English literary history,[38] but the influence on subsequent English poetry he attributed to this poem was contested by John Lehmann: "Considering the barrier that the Scots vernacular forms for most Southern Englishmen, it is unlikely that MacDiarmid's actual influence can have been anything more than slight."[39] It would of course be an exaggeration to describe these Southern Englishmen as insular. Their interests did not extend so far as the island they inhabited.

"Scarcely any critics have written on him," A. Alvarez complained when MacDiarmid's *Collected Poems* arrived for review at the *Observer*, not thinking to draw upon Mr. Wain's knowledge of Hungarian. It was clearly fortunate for him that the *Festschrift* had also arrived, but-nearly all of its fifteen contributors were Scots. Or, as he chose to put it: "no comment by outsiders is included".[40]

Once the poet's politics had been duly denounced and his incomprehensible dislike of the English disposed of, his *Collected Poems* were, however, well received. The difficulty for the English critics, understandably enough, was to show that their favourable reception of the poems was well founded. To take a fairly representative example: the basically sympathetic review by Donald Davie was weakened by a tendentious yoking together of MacDiarmid with English writers, his earlier lyrics being associated with Hardy, and "Dìreadh III" with, of all things, Wordsworth's lines "When to the Attractions of the Busy World."[41]

In recent years there has been a tendency to give MacDiarmid a mention in English literary studies of his period, rather than ignoring him altogether as before, and some space has been found for his poems in some of the anthologies. Even the controversy about "Perfect" attracted more than moral fervour. In his expanded edition of Michael Roberts' *Faber Book of Modern Verse* (1965), the American anthologist Donald Hall included that newly notorious poem along with seven others by MacDiarmid—the Scots ones unglossed, in a notable gesture of optimism.

The publication of the Penguin *Selected Poems* (1970), and the reissue of this volume despite the arrival of another paperback selection, *The Hugh MacDiarmid Anthology*, marked what must surely be a significant turning-point in terms of active readership. And this was consolidated by the inclusion of MacDiarmid in an Open University course on Twentieth Century Poetry (1976). The supreme contemporary accolade came in 1978 with a feature in a colour supplement.

But no notable English critic or scholar has yet published anything substantial or well-informed about MacDiarmid's work. If in 1962 the critics had little to say of the *Collected Poems* that could lend conviction to their judgments, sixteen years later, with the publication of the two volumes of *Complete Poems*, there was little beyond the occasional comments of Anthony Burgess to suggest any advance in that direction. Indeed, Derek Mahon felt it necessary when reviewing the *Complete Poems* to explain to his readers that he was neither an Englishman nor a Scotsman, and hence able, he said, "to read the poems, whether in English or in Scots (a perfectly straightforward task, despite their supposedly comic impenetrability) without preconceptions or polemical interference, and conclude that their author was a poet of the very first rank, comparable with Pasternak and Neruda, Eliot and Seferis."[42]

In his last years it became received practice to refer to MacDiarmid as "a great Scotsman" or "a major Scottish poet." His life and work rest on the proposition that these words should mean, or come to mean, in the mouths of those who use them, neither more nor less than "a great man, a major poet."

REFERENCES

1. *S.E.J.*, 16 Jan. 1925, p. 66.
2. "The National Party," *M.S.*, Jan. 1931, pp. 25–9.
3. Letter from MacDiarmid to H.B. Cruickshank, 10 Oct. 1930.
4. "A Poet Runs Amok," *D.R.,* 24 Sept. 1930.
5. "Peteleon," "Blasphemy and Divine Philosophy Mixed," *S.O.*, 2 Oct. 1930, p. 12.
6. "Two Views of Hugh MacDiarmid's New Poem," *D.R.*, 29 Oct. 1930.
7. *S.O.*, 24 Dec. 1931, p. 11.
8. "The Present Work of Hugh MacDiarmid," *S.O.*, 22 Dec. 1932.
9. "Modern Scots Poetry," in *Edinburgh Essays on Scots Literature*, Edinburgh 1933, pp. 126–48.
10. "Readers and Writers," *N.A.*, 15 Nov. 1923, pp. 32–3.
11. *Criterion*, April 1931, pp. 516–20.
12. "Literature in Scotland," *Spectator*, 25 May 1934, p. 823.
13. "Literature from 1910 to 1935," *Sc.*, 6 May 1935.
14. "A Literature without a Language," *Outlook*, June 1936.
15. *Scott and Scotland*, London 1936, pp. 19, 20, 21–2.
16. *The Present Age from 1914*, London 1939, pp. 115–16.
17. "A unique Scots Poet," *Sc.*, 11 Aug. 1962.
18. "Hugh MacDiarmid: The Poet at Seventy," *G.H.*, 11 Aug. 1962.

19. K. Buthlay, *Hugh MacDiarmid (C. M. Grieve)*, Edinburgh 1964. D. Glen, *Hugh MacDiarmid (Christopher Murray Grieve) and the Scottish Renaissance*, Edinburgh 1964.

20. *Literature in my Time*, London 1933, p. 240.

21. "Le Groupe de 'La Renaissance écossaise,'" *R.A.*, Apr. 1924, pp. 295–307.

22. "La Renaissance écossaise," *N.R.*, June-July 1924, pp. 116–17. (Also *Marsyas*, Sept. 1924.)

23. "Hugh MacDiarmid: Visionnaire du langage," *Critique*, Dec. 1955, pp. 1056–63.

24. "Literature and Life," *I.S.*, 8 Jan. 1927, pp. 431–33.

25. Letter to the author, 4 Sept. 1951.

26. *Englische Studien*, 67,3 (1933), pp. 371–90.

27. *New Scots Renascence*, Düren, 1958.

28. J. Szili, "Hugh MacDiarmid Költeszete," *Filológiai Közlöny*, 5 (Dec. 1959), pp. 379–98; 6 (June 1960), pp. 37–66.

29. *Guardian*, 28 Feb. 1962, p. 8.

30. J. Levy, "Skotsky regionalismus v povalecne britske literature," *Casopis Pro Moderni Filologii*, 34 (1951), pp. 151–55. J. Kocmanová, "Art and Revolution in the Poetry of Hugh MacDiarmid," *Philologica Pragensia*, 5 (1962), pp. 218–25. G. Bidwell, "MacDiarmid," *Tworczósc*, Summer 1956, pp. 202–4. V. S. Vakhrushev, "Stikhi o Lenine Mak-Daiarmide," *Nauchnye Dokledy Vysshei Shkoly*, 5, pp. 68–79.

31. "Hugh MacDiarmid," *Sewanee Review*, Jan.-Mar. 1940, pp. 105–18.

32. "Hugh MacDiarmid and Scottish Poetry," *Poetry* (Chicago), July 1948, pp. 202–18.

33. "Hugh MacDiarmid: The Marxist Messiah," *Prairie Schooner*, Fall 1952, pp. 325–35.

34. *The Modern Poets*, New York, 1960, pp. 131–36.

35. *New York Times*, 25 Feb. 1962.

36. "Hugh MacDiarmid: Hailing Us All," *Poetry*, June 1963, pp. 177–81.

37. "Hugh MacDiarmid," *Scrutiny*, Dec. 1935, p. 305.

38. *A Hope for Poetry*, Oxford 1934, pp. 51, 53.

39. "Some Revolutionary Trends in English Poetry 1930–1935," *International Literature*, Apr. 1936, pp. 60–69.

40. "Dialect and the Dialectic," *Observer*, 12 Aug. 1962.

41. "A'e Gowden Lyric," *N.S.*, 10 Aug. 1962.

42. "Lament for the Makar," *N.S.*, 1 Dec. 1978.

SELECT BIBLIOGRAPHY

Principal Works by Hugh MacDiarmid (C. M. Grieve)

Annals of the Five Senses. Montrose 1923; Edinburgh 1930.
Sangschaw. Edinburgh 1925.
Penny Wheep. Edinburgh 1926.
A Drunk Man Looks at the Thistle. Edinburgh 1926; Glasgow 1953; Edinburgh 1956; Edinburgh 1962; Falkland 1969; ed. J. C. Weston, Amherst 1971.
Contemporary Scottish Studies. London 1926; enlarged edn., Edinburgh 1976.
Albyn, or Scotland and the Future. London 1927.
To Circumjack Cencrastus, or The Curly Snake. Edinburgh 1930.
First Hymn to Lenin and Other Poems. London 1931.
Scots Unbound and Other Poems. Stirling 1932.
Scottish Scene. (With Lewis Grassic Gibbon.) London 1934; Bath 1974.
Stony Limits and Other Poems. London 1934.
At the Sign of the Thistle: a Collection of Essays. London [1934].
Second Hymn to Lenin and Other Poems. London 1935.
Scottish Eccentrics. London 1936; New York 1972.
The Islands of Scotland. London and New York 1939.
Lucky Poet. London 1943; London 1972.
A Kist of Whistles. Glasgow [1947].
In Memoriam James Joyce. Glasgow 1955.
Stony Limits and Scots Unbound and Other Poems. Edinburgh 1956.
The Battle Continues. Edinburgh 1957.
Burns Today and Tomorrow. Edinburgh 1959.
The Kind of Poetry I Want. Edinburgh 1961.
Collected Poems. New York 1962; revised edn., 1967.
The Company I've Kept. London 1966.
A Lap of Honour. London 1967.
A Clyack-Sheaf. London 1969.
More Collected Poems. London 1970.
Complete Poems 1920–1976. Ed. M. Grieve & W. R. Aitken. 2 vols. London 1978.

Selections

Selected Poems of Hugh MacDiarmid. Ed. R. Crombie Saunders. Glasgow 1944.
Speaking for Scotland. Baltimore 1946.

The Uncanny Scot: A Selection of Prose by Hugh MacDiarmid. Ed. K. Buthlay.
    London 1968.
Selected Essays of Hugh MacDiarmid. Ed. D. Glen. London 1969.
Selected Poems. Ed. D. Craig & J. Manson. Harmondsworth 1970.
The Hugh MacDiarmid Anthology. Ed. M. Grieve & A. Scott. London 1972.
The Socialist Poems of Hugh MacDiarmid. Ed. T. S. Law & T. Berwick.
    London 1978.

Recordings

Hugh MacDiarmid Reads his own Poetry. Dublin: Claddagh Records, 1969.
A Drunk Man Looks at the Thistle: Hugh MacDiarmid Reads his own Poem.
    Dublin: Claddagh Records, 1970.
Poems of Hugh MacDiarmid. With commentary by K. Buthlay. 2 cassettes.
    Glasgow: Scotsoun Cassettes, 1976.
Whaur Extremes Meet. Alton: Tuatha Music, 1979.

Criticism

Agenda. Double Issue: Hugh MacDiarmid and Scottish Poetry.
    Autumn–Winter 1967–68.
Aitken, Mary Baird. 'The Poetry of Hugh MacDiarmid.' *Scottish Art and
    Letters*, 4 (1949), 5–25.
Akros. Special Hugh MacDiarmid Issue. April 1970.
——. Special Double Hugh MacDiarmid Issue. August 1977.
Buthlay, Kenneth. *Hugh MacDiarmid (C. M. Grieve).* Edinburgh 1964.
——. 'The Appreciation of the Golden Lyric: Early Scots Poems of
    Hugh MacDiarmid.' *Scottish Literary Journal*, July 1975, 41–66.
Craig, David. *The Real Foundations.* London 1973.
Daiches, David. 'Hugh MacDiarmid and Scottish Poetry.' *Poetry*
    (Chicago), July 1948, 202–18.
——. 'Introduction,' *A Drunk Man Looks at the Thistle* by Hugh MacDiar-
    mid. Glasgow 1953; Edinburgh 1956 and 1962.
——. 'MacDiarmid's New Poem.' *Lines Review*, August 1955, 22–26.
Deutsch, Babette. *Poetry in Our Time.* New York 1952.
Duval, K. D., and Smith, Sydney Goodsir, editors. *Hugh MacDiarmid: a
    Festschrift.* Edinburgh 1962.
Glen, Duncan. *Hugh MacDiarmid (Christopher Murray Grieve) and the
    Scottish Renaissance.* Edinburgh 1964.
——, editor. *Hugh MacDiarmid: a Critical Survey.* Edinburgh 1972.
Glicksberg, Charles I. 'Hugh MacDiarmid: the Marxist Messiah.'
    Prairie Schooner, Fall 1952, 325–35.
Lindsay, Maurice. *History of Scottish Literature.* London 1977.
McQuillan, Ruth. 'MacDiarmid's Other Dictionary.' *Lines Review*, Sep-
    tember 1978, 5–14.
——, and Shearer, Agnes. *In Line with the Ramna Stacks*, Edinburgh 1980.
Morgan, Edwin. *Essays.* Cheadle 1974.

——. *Hugh MacDiarmid*. Harlow 1976.

Muir, Edwin. *Scott and Scotland*. London 1936.

Perrie, Walter. 'Nietzsche and the Drunk Man.' *Cencrastus*, Spring 1980, 9–12.

Rosenthal, M.L.. *The Modern Poets*. New York 1960.

Saunders, R. Crombie. 'The Thistle in the Lion's Mouth.' *Life and Letters To-day*, March 1945, 147–55.

Saurat, Denis. 'Le Groupe de "La Renaissance Ecossaise."' *Revue Anglo-Américaine*, April 1924, 295–307.

Scott, P. H., and Davis, A. C., editors. *The Age of MacDiarmid: Essays on Hugh MacDiarmid and his Influence on Contemporary Scotland*. Edinburgh 1980.

Scottish Literary Journal. MacDiarmid Memorial Number. December 1978.

Soutar, William. 'The Poetry of Hugh MacDiarmid.' *Free Man*, 7 April 1934, 8–9.

Southworth, James G. *Sowing the Spring*. Oxford 1940.

Watson, Roderick B. *Hugh MacDiarmid*. (Open University Course Unit.) Milton Keynes 1976.

Weston, John C. *Hugh MacDiarmid's 'A Drunk Man Looks at the Thistle:' an Essay*. Preston 1970.